William Shillinglaw Crockett

In Praise of Tweed

William Shillinglaw Crockett

In Praise of Tweed

ISBN/EAN: 9783744694728

Printed in Europe, USA, Canada, Australia, Japan

Cover: Foto ©Lupo / pixelio.de

More available books at **www.hansebooks.com**

..IN..
PRAISE OF TWEED

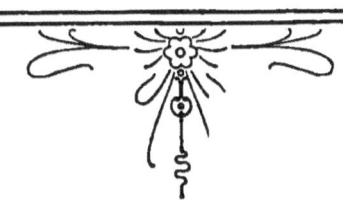

CROCKETT
MINISTER OF TWEEDSMUIR

AUTHOR OF 'MINSTRELSY OF THE MERSE'
'A BERWICKSHIRE BARD' &c.

SELKIRK
JAMES LEWIS
1899

TO ALL

BOTH NEAR AND FAR FOR WHOM

THE TWEED

HAS A KINDLY MEMORY

"*Morning rose on the blue waters of Tuctha.*"
"*The stream of Tuetha rolled in its pride.*"—OSSIAN.

"*And I'll awa to bonnie Tweedside,
And see my dearie come through.*"—ALLAN RAMSAY.

"*The Tweed, pure parent-stream,
Whose pastoral banks first heard my Doric reed.*"—
                                              JAMES THOMSON.

"*Up stately wimpling Tweed I've sped.*"
"*Yarrow and Tweed to monie a tune ower Scotland rings.*"—
                                              ROBERT BURNS.

"*The ever-dear Tweed, whose waters flow continually through my heart, and make me often greet in my lonely evenings.*"—
                                              THOMAS AIRD.

"*Which of the world's streams can Tweed envy, with its beauty and renown?*"—GEORGE BORROW.

"*'T was ours by pastoral Tweed to wind
Through the Arcadia of the Borderland.*"—D. M. MOIR (Delta).

"*My cradle song, nor other hymn
I'd choose, nor gentler requiem dear
Than Tweed's, that through death's twilight dim,
Mourned in the latest minstrel's ear.*"—ANDREW LANG.

"*Both are good, the streams of north and south, but he who has given his heart to the Tweed, as did Tyro, in Homer, to the Enipeus, will never change his love.*"—ANDREW LANG.

PREFACE.

IN the arrangement of material for another work of Border interest, it occurred to me that the Tweed might well be made to contribute its quota to anthological literature. Thus the present book has come into being, and is sent forth in the hope that it may prove a source of pleasure to each of its readers — to those who carry with them many a kindly memory of Tweedside, and those also who have not yet felt, from personal association, the wondrous charms of the storied stream. Few rivers have been more besung than the Tweed, and there are few worthier of the minstrel's art. So long as Tweed flows seaward, the singer's praise will not cease. It will be as true of Tweed as of Yarrow—

> And summer's flowers shall linger yet,
>   Where all thy mossy margins guide thee;
> And minstrels, met as we have met,
>   Shall sit and sing their songs beside thee.

PREFACE.

A word of thanks is due to those living writers who have graced this volume with their contributions. So many verses 'in praise of Tweed' have been penned that one could not but experience a difficulty in the somewhat delicate business of choice and rejection. I desire specially to mention Mr Ruskin, Mr Andrew Lang, and Mr J. Logie Robertson, who at once gave me their consent to reprint what appears at their respective names. I am also under obligation to a large number of publishers for liberty to use many of the poems that follow. The illustrations are from the well-known Leadervale engraving works of Messrs M. & T. Scott, Edinburgh.

W. S. C.

TWEEDSMUIR,
Christmas, 1898.

Sir Walter Scott.

CONTENTS.

		PAGE
INTRODUCTION		xv.–xxxix.
I.	SIR ROBERT AYTON	3
	Sonnet to the Tweed	5
II.	LORD YESTER	6
	Tweedside	7
III.	ROBERT CRAWFORD	8
	Tweedside	9
IV.	WILLIAM HAMILTON OF BANGOUR	11
	The Seasons on Tweedside	13
V.	DR JOHN LANGHORNE	16
	From Genius and Valour	17
VI.	MRS JOHN HUNTER	19
	Farewell to Tweedside	20
VII.	JAMES HOOK	21
	The Banks of Tweed	22
VIII.	ROBERT FERGUSSON	23
	The Tweed (from "The Rivers of Scotland")	25
	The Tweed (from "Hame Content")	26
IX.	ANDREW SCOTT	28
	Marriage of the Tweed and Teviot	29
X.	WILLIAM WORDSWORTH	31
	Sonnet composed at Neidpath Castle	39
XI.	SIR WALTER SCOTT	40
	November on Tweedside	43
	November on Tweedside (and on Yarrow)	45

	December on Tweedside .	47
	Christmas on Tweedside .	48
XII.	JOHN LEYDEN	52
	The Tweed at Kelso . . .	54
XIII.	PROFESSOR JOHN WILSON (CHRISTOPHER NORTH)	55
	The Tweed at Tweedsmuir . .	57
XIV.	JOHN ALEXANDER PRINGLE . .	63
	A Dream of Tweedside . .	63
XV.	D. M. MOIR (DELTA)	65
	Dryburgh Abbey	66
XVI.	HENRY SCOTT RIDDELL . . .	67
	Bonnie Tweedside . . .	69
XVII.	W. A. FOSTER	71
	The Bonnie Tweed for Me .	71
	Away to the Tweed . .	73
XVIII.	ALEXANDER HUME	74
	The Tweed	75
	The Braes o' Tweeddale . . .	75
XIX.	T. T. STODDART	77
	Tweed for Ever . . .	78
	An Angler's Rambles . .	79
	Tweed and Its Prospects . .	80
	To the Tweed . . .	82
XX.	DR JOHN BROWN	84
	Something about a Well . . .	85
XXI.	GEORGE PAULIN	87
	The Tweed Revisited . .	88
	The Tweed at Abbotsford .	89
XXII.	JOHN RUSKIN	91
	The Tweed	92
XXIII.	W. FORSYTH	95
	The Tweed . . .	59

XXIV.	DR WALTER C. SMITH	99
	Dryburgh	100
XXV.	C. M. DAWSON	101
	The Tweed at Coldstream	101
	The Tweed Revisited	104
XXVI.	PROFESSOR VEITCH	106
	The Tweed	108
	The Tweed (from "The Tweed and Other Poems")	109
XXVII.	ALEXANDER SMITH	115
	At Peebles	117
XXVIII.	JOHN TOD	119
	Tweedle-dum and Tweedle-dee	120
XXIX.	J. B. SELKIRK	122
	Where Tweed flows down	123
XXX.	JOHN DICKSON	124
	Bonnie Tweed	124
XXXI.	A. G. (from "Blackwood's Magazine")	126
	To the River Tweed	126
XXXII.	ALEXANDER BROWN	128
	At Neidpath	128
	At Melrose	130
XXXIII.	JOHN SMART, R.S.A., R.S.W.	132
	A Day by the Tweed	133
XXXIV.	ANDREW LANG	134
	Twilight on Tweed	136
	Ballade of the Tweed	137
	April on Tweed	138
XXXV.	ALEXANDER ANDERSON	140
	When first I saw the Tweed	142
XXXVI.	"EFFIE" WILLIAMSON	144
	A Summer Day's Drive	145
	Spring by Tweedside	147

CONTENTS.

XXXVII.	J. Logie Robertson	149
	Summer Gloaming on Tweedside	150
	The Tweed	151
XXXVIII.	Rev. John Buchan	152
	The Tweed	152
	Tweed and Yarrow	153
	An Autumn Thought	154
	Voices of the Tweed	155
	Tweedsmuir	155
	Neidpath at Eventide	156
XXXIX.	James L. Hercus	158
	The Tweed	159
XL.	Duncan Fraser	160
	The Tweed—a Rhapsody	160
	A First Day by the Tweed	162
XLI.	W. Sanderson	164
	A Dream of Tweed	164
	Nae wunner Tweed's remembered	166
XLII.	W. Cuthbertson	168
	Berwick Bay	169
	Dryburgh	171
XLIII.	Anon	173
	The Silver Tweed	173
XLIV.	James Mabon	175
	Tweed and Yarrow	175
	Twilight on Tweed	176
	Springtide on Tweed	178
	The Valley Path	179
XLV.	W. Alexander	180
	The Tweed	180
XLVI.	W. S. Crockett	182
	At Tweed's Well	182
	The Tweed	183
	The Secret of Tweed	184

ILLUSTRATIONS.

Sir Walter Scott	*Frontispiece.*	
Lord Yester	*Facing Page*	6
Robert Fergusson, Hamilton of Bangour, Andrew Scott, William Wordsworth	,,	16
John Leyden	,,	52
Professor John Wilson, D. M. Moir, H. S. Riddell, W. A. Foster	,,	64
T. T. Stoddart, Dr John Brown, George Paulin, John Ruskin	,,	80
William Forsyth, Walter C. Smith, C. M. Dawson, Professor Veitch	,,	96
Alexander Smith, John Tod, J. B. Selkirk, John Dickson	,,	112
Andrew Lang	,,	134
Alexander Brown, John Smart, Alexander Anderson, J. Logie Robertson	,,	144
"Effie," Rev. John Buchan, J. L. Hercus, Duncan Fraser	,,	160
William Cuthbertson, William Sanderson, James Mabon, W. S. Crockett	,,	176

INTRODUCTION.

THERE are probably few people who will question the statement that the Tweed is the river most of all associated with Scottish romance. Were it only for the sake of Sir Walter, and the imperishable memories of Ashestiel and Abbotsford, that would surely be sufficient evidence for a statement the truth of which seems so apparent. But, apart from Scott and his Tweedside life, the Tweed has other memories and associations which draw us to it, and single it out as being the most noteworthy of Scottish streams. It is perhaps not too much to speak of the Tweed as the national river. It is certainly the best known to the stranger who visits our shores; and when playing the rôle of foreigner ourselves, we may be asked about the Tweed, and hear of it again and again, whilst comparatively little mention is made of the other rivers in our country. What the Rhine is to the German, and the Jordan was to the Jew, it seems quite natural to say that the Tweed is to the Scot. Into its hundred miles of water-way there has been crowded more of the elements of the historical and the traditional than can be said of any stream of similar proportions. Story and song flourish by its banks as nowhere else in the kingdom. And in richness of natural beauty, for continuous and striking variety of the most enchanting scenery, Tweedside has few rivals, and fewer still to surpass it. Not indeed that the other Scottish rivers have not been dowered with fineness of scenery, or that they are lacking in fulness of romance. That could never be said of a country whose physical beauty is a wide world's admiration, and to the extent of whose literary treasures all eyes have been attracted; yet, somehow or other, the valley of the Tweed appears to hold the premier place in the national sentiment as the home-land of national romance, and the place where so much of the patriotic spirit has centred itself. Of

INTRODUCTION. xvii.

course, this is owing, to a very large degree, to the genius of him who, more than any man, has glorified and immortalised the Tweed. The Tweed could not have been otherwise than Scott's favourite river. To him no music sounded so sweetly as Tweed gurgling over its stony bed. From source to sea he knew its every bend and flow. That silver line, issuing from the heart of the southern hills, bounding along past a hundred scenes famous in story, and gliding softly at last into Old Ocean's arms, was to him the most winsome stretch of countryside in all the world.

And there are many who share the same feelings—to whom other feelings would be impossible — whose recollections go back on long years of joy by the fair river, close knit to their hearts through the most tender and hallowed ties. And there are very many, also, even amongst those who have not known Tweedside from residential interest or ancestral association, to whom its name must always be the embodiment of the most splendid poetry, and the synonym for the most soul-stirring and fascinating of old-world lore. For it is not the river as a mere accumulation of waters drawn from every Border glen and hillside that constitutes the "ever-dear Tweed," not its nooks of bosky beauty, not the marvels of colouring that come with the changing seasons in the lavish adornment of its banks, not even from the piscatorial side of human vision, agreeable though that mostly is, would we so judge Tweed ; but because every league of its course is laden with the choicest treasures of our national life — the legends, and ballads, and songs; all the unpriced wealth of that deathless romance and glamourie which has helped so much to make the literature of Scotland great and world-honoured. Short of this

> The Tweed were as poor as the Amazon,
> That, for all the years it has roll'd,
> Can tell but how fair was the morning red,
> How sweet the evening gold.

An important factor in this pre-eminence of

Tweedside cannot be overlooked in the fact of its natural situation. For many centuries the march-line between two hostile kingdoms, the Tweed has shared in the experience, common to every part of the Border country, of the wild and lawless spirit of those rough raiding days. Chiefly from this cause is it that much of the early poetry of the Borders is what it is—a ballad minstrelsy of rugged and homely rhyme, shrining the memory of many a doughty deed, and of many a heart-crushing sorrow. For the most pronounced pathos in the midst of word-pictures, inimitable in their weirdness and uncouthness, and with all the tragedy and pallor of the battle-field about them, few things can compare with these crude products of a past age. It were inevitable in a condition of things where the spirit of rivalry, of determined daring, of mastery, was rampant, and yet withal where often the kindlier and gentler passions asserted themselves even in the rudest and coarsest types, for the poetic temperament to declare itself, and to hand down to these later days this rich song and ballad legacy. From the recital of such old-time deeds, desperate enough, in all conscience, as they were in many instances, and in others, deep throbbing with the power that melts to tears, are we now gathering the sweeter fruits of a more peaceful poesy. And the influence which it sheds is no less magnetic in binding us to that portion of the country in whose welfare we are chiefly interested, and that holds the first place in our affections.

The poetry of Tweedside has changed with the changing characteristics of the district. The natural features of the Tweed valley have altered in great measure since the epoch of blood and iron. The river is largely the same; only here and there does it flow in a different channel. But the out-lying landways have undergone a beautiful and beneficent metamorphosis. The 'derkesome forests' have disappeared. What are now peaceful pasture-lands and long stretches of richly cultivated soil, in those 'far-off times of

INTRODUCTION. xxi.

roaming and of raiding,' would echo with 'the cry of hart and hind and dae and rae and of a' wild bestis that roamed in grete plentie through the many semelie trees.' But the huntsman's horn has sounded its requiem. And the era of the sword has passed. Not now returning forayers 'fill the hall with revel, wassail-rout, and brawl.' The castle on the crag is a roofless ruin, exposed to all the elements, and crumbling to dissolution. Never a knight rides forth in helmet plumed with his lady's favour. The battle-din is silent. The clansman's voice is long since stilled. Tweed —kindly old Tweed, barrier and divider between generations sunk in the dust of ages, seals both Borders in a blessed and holy union. And enough one Flodden!

Thus the songs that have sprung into being by the banks of the Tweed are in the main of a quietly reflective and pastoral character, in sweet correspondence with the natural features of the district. The scenery of the river has been grandly imaged in many of these placid and love-born compositions. No one could have put it more eloquently or with truer artistic grace, than has John Veitch, of beloved memory. "The songs of the Tweed contain the most explicit references to the scenery, and show an increasing appreciation of that softer side of nature which appears in the valley of the river. For, while the wildest, grandest, and most secluded of the scenery is to be found among the great hills, and in the glens of the waters and the burns, the softest, the most cultured and beautiful, lies in the valley of the Tweed. You may see there, in the summer time, the gleaming flow, and hear the music, by day and night, of a river clear as the light of heaven. Its motion is poetry itself, as it now stays calm in pool, and then rushes bright and joyous in stream. There are green haughs, soft meadows, and corn-fields, and gently sloping hill-sides, and many parts well and picturesquely wooded—all looking as if the human life there were pleasant and comfortable. It is in this region that we find the source of the Border love-songs in the seventeenth century; and they grow increasingly in sympathy with the green haughs, the sunny gleam, and the gentle murmur of the river, the notes of early birds, the bleating of lambs, and the melancholy music of the sequestered cushat of the woods in the vale of Tweed. In the earlier songs this influence is to a great extent an unconscious one. The singer felt, but did not dwell on the aspects of the scenery, which yet coincided with the passion he sought to express. The sympathy he had for the nature around him was subordinate to and illustrative of that primal emotion—human love. We yet see that the sense of the gentle beauty in things lay deep down in his heart; and, like the burn that flows hidden under the grassy fringe and nourishes the verdure of the glen, helped to sustain the lightsome life of many a song. And we have only to come down to the more modern period of Robert Crawford, to find how profuse was the feeling for nature that was mingled with the expression of passion; and to the later times of Leyden, Hogg, Scott, and others, to observe the depth and directness of sympathy for the hills, glens, and streams of the Border land. This was the new element in the poetry of the Borders; and it was from its rise and spread in the district that the fresh breath of nature passed into the Scottish, and, we may add, the English, poetry of this century."[1]

Men and women of all conditions in life have come under this magic spell of the Tweed. And for all who breathe the pure and sweet atmosphere of song, Tweed is the kindest of nursing mothers. The pages that follow will be ample proof of this. But while there are so many who have thus sung of the enchanted land of the Tweed, whose compositions are a part of the stable literature of the country, there are also many who, if they have not specially apostrophised the romantic river, have, nevertheless,

---

[1] *History and Poetry of the Scottish Border*, vol. ii. 225-6.

borne a willing witness to its inspiring influence. Addison, in an early *Spectator*, has one or two references to the Tweed and the Border country. James Thomson, the Poet of The Seasons, spent his boyhood by its wooded braes within one of its most charming nooks, and there cannot be a doubt but that much of his power and truthfulness as a word-painter is traceable to this period.

"And here awhile the muse,
High hovering o'er the broad cerulean scene,
    Sees Caledonia, in romantic view ;
Her airy mountains, from the waving main,
    Invested with a keen diffusive sky—
Breathing the soul acute; her forests huge,
    Incult, robust, and tall, by Nature's hand
    Planted of old; her azure lakes between,
    Poured out extensive, and of watery wealth
    Full ; winding, deep, and green, her fertile vales
With many a cool, translucent, brimming flood
Washed lovely, from the Tweed (pure parent stream
Whose pastoral banks first heard my Doric reed,
    With silvan Jed, thy tributary brook),
To where the north-inflated tempest foams
    O'er Orca's or Betubium's highest peak."

Thomson is said to have written his 'Winter'

at Dryburgh, and the following may easily be descriptive of the Tweed in flood :—

> " Wide o'er the brim, with many a torrent swelled,
> And the mixed ruin of its banks o'erspread,
> At last the roused-up river pours along ;
> Resistless, roaring, dreadful, down it comes
> From the rude mountain and the mossy wild—
> Tumbling through rocks abrupt and sounding far ;
> Then o'er the sanded valley floating spreads,
> Calm, sluggish, silent ; till again, constrained
> Between two meeting hills, it bursts away,
> Where rocks and woods o'erhang the turbid stream ;
> There, gathering triple force, rapid and deep,
> It boils, and wheels, and foams, and thunders through."

And there are other passages in his poems strongly suggestive of Tweedside scenery. One of these, 'Of a Country Life,' written when a student at Edinburgh University, is singularly pleasing, and highly characteristic of the sweet vale of 'soft meandering Tweed.'

The upper reaches of the Tweed were a familiar happy hunting-ground to Thomas Campbell, and many a rollicking evening the author of *The Pleasures of Hope* enjoyed at Hamilton Paul's hospitable manse of Broughton. To Kit North and his congenial coterie, next to a night at "Tibbie's," was the pleasure of an excursion down the Meggat, across the Linns of Talla into Tweeddale, with new friendships at the far-known Crook. Then became he indeed "beadsman of Tweedside." Some of Wordsworth's dearest memories lingered around Tweedside, and gave force to his pen. Thomas Aird's remark is replete with such pathos as only a Tweedside man can interpret—"The ever-dear Tweed whose waters flow continually through my heart, and make me often *greet* in my lonely evenings." When George Borrow — Lavengro — first visited Scotland, he tells us that at the sight of the Tweed he was so affected that he wept with admiration. It is a regret that Burns gave the Tweed no song all to itself, yet his poetic soul was fired with the beauty of the noble river. Many a time must he have driven down Tweedside on the rumbling stage-coach of the day, making its way by the Devil's Beef Tub and Tweedshaws to the Beild and Broughton, then on to Edinburgh through the winding hill-roads, rough, bare, and shelterless. One song of Burns's connects his name with this portion of the Tweed—Lincumdoddie. Here dwelt Willie Wastle and his fair spouse. Who does not remember the inimitable portrait which the poet has drawn of "sic a wife as Willie had?" James Hogg, *the* Shepherd of the Ettrick hills, was a familiar figure on Tweedside, but he has not left any special composition in praise of the river. His nephew, Robert Hogg of Stobo, a bright star set all too quickly, would doubtless have added fresh glory to the Tweed, had his life been prolonged. One of the finest ballads of the Tweed—*The Tweeddale Raid*—is from his pen, and is an admirable certificate of his genius. Thomas Smibert, the poet-physician of Peebles, and Robert Chambers, eminent publisher and large-souled patriot, have more than one mention of their native stream as seen at Peebles and Abbotsford. So have James Nicol and Hamilton

Paul, the poet-preachers of Traquair and Broughton. A composition of the latter divine is a special favourite in the district of its birth. It is included here for the first time in a verse collection.

> How charming are the banks of Tweed
>   When smiles the blooming year,
> How sweet to tread the flowery mead
>   When summer days are near;
> To visit Talla's Waterfa',
>   Or roam along the brook,
> And then to spend an hour or twa
>   Wi' Jeanie o' the Crook.
>
> How happy be the favoured youth,
>   When roaming on Tweedside,
> Shall hear frae lovely Jeanie's mouth
>   'O, I will be your bride.'
> And I, as many a beau, advance
>   And catch a wistfu' look,
> In hopes to catch a kindly glance
>   Frae Jeanie o' the Crook.
>
> Could I licht on some sheltered spot
>   Amang the hills so green,
> Where I might rear a rural cot
>   To harbour me and Jean!
> Or could I in yon bonnie glen
>   Find out some cosy nook,
> Where I in joy my life might spen'
>   Wi' Jeanie o' the Crook.
>
> But wae's my heart, the days are gane
>   The days that I ha'e seen,

> I aince had hope, now I ha'e nane,
>   For hark ! the words o' Jean :
> " If ye be wise, take my advice—
>   Gang hame and mind your book,
> For O ! dear Paul, ye 're far owre aul'
>   For Jeanie o' the Crook."

Jean Logan Watson, a sweet authoress, born at Broughton Place, the abode of the Secretary Murray, whilst writing touchingly of by-gone days in a Border village, did not forget that the Tweed flowed near, and rippling past the old castle of Drumelzier, thrilled her with its matchless melody. James Sanderson, an Earlston weaver, sang as he drove his shuttle and thread, two beautiful stanzas on "The banks and braes o' bonnie Tweed."

> "Ye banks and braes o' bonnie Tweed,
>   Ye seem aye clad in summer's green ;
> Where spring's first early flowers are spread,
>   And where the last o' summer's seen.
>
> "Oft have I wandered by thy side
>   To hear thy gushing waters play,
> And list the mavis woo his bride,
>   And sing the e'ening sun away."

Nor was pawky John Younger of St Boswells, angler, essayist, philosopher, behind his friend in invoking the genius of the noble stream. The eccentric laird of Dryburgh Abbey, the eleventh Earl of Buchan, wooed the lyric muse under its classic shade as did also his son, Sir David Erskine. Dr Alexander Geddes, chaplain in the family of the sixth Earl of Traquair, and author, among others, of the well-known Jacobite lyric, *Lewie Gordon*, wrote, at Traquair House, *Linton, a Tweeddale Pastoral*, on the occasion of the birth of a son and heir to the noble house, wherein are some local allusions to the Tweed. Washington Irving came under the spell of the river during his visit to Scott at Abbotsford in the early years of the century, and his countrymen are to-day among the devoutest worshippers at the shrines of the great Wizard. The *Songs of the Edinburgh Angling Club*, whose headquarters at The Nest, just opposite Ashestiel, has been the scene of many a jovial hour, are full of references to the richness of the scenery at this particular point, and the pleasure that comes from plying the 'gentle art' in so romantic a locality. Let one suffice:

INTRODUCTION.

The sun glints over Neidpath Fell,
   And lights the forest grey;
The dewdrop glistens on the grass,
   The cock proclaims the day.
Then up, my lads! cast care aside,
   Throw business to the deil;
We'll fill our baskets frae yon stream
   That winds by Ashestiel.

Let others toil frae day to day,
   This warl's gear to win,
Or seek in pleasure's vain pursuit,
   For joys they ne'er can fin';
But gie to me my weel worn creel,
   My ain rod in my han',
And tho' I'm poor, I envy not
   The noblest in the lan'.

What tho' my locks are lyart grown,
   And age has dimmed my e'e,
Wi' steady aim and skilful han'
   I yet can throw a flee.
The angler's heart can ne'er grow auld,
   Or aught o' grief retain;
Ance mair beside the sunny stream,
   And he is young again.

When head and han' are tired alike
   Wi' wark that kens nae rest;
When care sits cowerin' on the heart,
   And life has lost its zest;

> The balmy breeze upon my cheek,
>   The gowan on the lea,
> The saft sough o' the limber rod
>   Aye gladness bring to me.

William Wye Smith, a Scoto-Canadian bard, sings sweetly of 'The Bonnie Land' of his fathers:

> Oh, weel I ken the bonnie land!
>   Beside the Tweed it lies;
> I ken the very nook o' the sky
>   'Neath which its pearls and gowans lie,
>   And where its mountains rise,
> Wi' Bemersyde and Cowdenknowes,
> Frae Newark Peel to the Loch o' the Lowes,
> Where laverocks sing and heather grows,
>   Oh, that's the bonnie land.

And there are many who will have no difficulty in sympathising with the writer of the following verses:

> This is the land where my fathers dwelt,
>   My fathers, long ago—
> The land of legend and of song,
>   Where the Tweed and the Yarrow flow.
>
> Here each hill and moor, each glen and glade,
>   Has its tale of stubborn fight;
> Here the Borderer bold, in days of old,
>   Stood for his country's right.

This is the glorious 'Land of Scott;'
  And I feel the mysterious spell
Of his wizard power, at the present hour,
  In my spirit strangely swell.

My home is now 'midst the Highland hills;
  Yet here by the Tweed I stand,
And, lifting my eye from its waters, I cry,
  'Hurrah for the Border Land!'

There is an exquisite and touching little poem of Scott's, which should have been inserted elsewhere—that written in the autumn of 1817, on the height north of Cauldshiels Loch, the western boundary of Abbotsford estate.

The sun upon the Weirdlaw hill,
  In Ettrick's vale is sinking sweet;
The westland wind is hushed and still—
  The lake lies sleeping at my feet.

Yet not the landscape to mine eye
  Bears those bright hues that once it bore;
Though evening, with her richest dye,
  Flames o'er the hills of Ettrick's shore.

With listless look along the plain,
  I see Tweed's silver current glide,
And coldly mark the holy fane
  Of Melrose rise in ruined pride.

> The quiet lake, the balmy air,
>   The hill, the stream, the tower, the tree,
> Are they still such as once they were,
>   Or is the dreary change in me?
>
> Alas, the warp'd and broken board,
>   How can it bear the painter's dye!
> The harp of strained and tuneless chord,
>   How to the minstrel's skill reply!
>
> To aching eye each landscape lowers,
>   To feverish pulse each gale blows chill;
> And Araby's or Eden's bowers
>   Were barren as this moorland hill.

Nor must we forget to mention dear, kindly John Campbell Shairp of *Bush aboon Traquair* immortality, whose Tweedside musings and Borderland wanderings are ever full of the tenderest recollections; or *ultimus Scotorum*, John Stuart Blackie, half-Tweedsider by birth, and a wholehearted Borderer from long acquaintance with the braes of Yarrow and the banks of Tweed. Professor Blackie never lost sight of his Border origin, the glens of his forefathers, or 'the soft Lowland tongue of the Borders.' He loved the musical rhythm of our common speech, and his most stirring songs are couched in native Doric *Merlin and Kentigern* is one of his best ballads, full of life and vigour, and all the pathos and tragedy of a dark and trying day. And lastly, all are familiar with Alison Rutherford's lines in *The Flowers of the Forest*, and there are quite a host of similar references in poetry that is not exclusively about the Tweed.

In prose literature, also, the Tweed has its due share of laudation. Sir Thomas Dick Lauder has done yeoman service for the Tweed in his *Scottish Rivers*; so did Pennecuik in his *Description of Tweeddale*, and William Chambers in his *History of Peeblesshire*. In many biographical and historical sketches — all of them pleasurable contributions to Border literature, the Tweed has had a well-merited recognition. Best of all has Professor Veitch thrown the strength of his philosophical insight and critical acumen and poetical fervour into that interpretation of the *History and Poetry of the Scottish Border* which must ever be associated with his name. Since the time of Sir Walter, no one has written more powerfully, or has sung more sweetly, of the heroic age of the Scottish Lowlands. All that Veitch did for his beloved Borders he adorned with a master hand, and hundreds are thankful to-day for such a life as his. It is not too much to style him, as has been done, the 'latter-day Scott,' and the 'Scottish Wordsworth.' His best memorial will be—not any erection of stone and lime placed in the street of his native town, or tablet in bronze on the walls of his University—but it will be the spirit of the man which glorified the scenes of Nature, and inspired not a few towards a tenderer love and a deeper attachment for everything that goes to make the Border country of Scotland the home of so much loving loyalty and honest pride in the furtherance of social and national well-being.

So that, looking back on all the long history of the Tweed, and remembering the important place which it holds in our life and literature, one is tempted to declare somewhat in the language of the old singer : " If I forget thee, O Tweed, let my right hand forget her cunning; if I do not remember thee, let my tongue cleave to the roof of my mouth." And sitting down by its banks, we begin to muse. Our hearts burn within us. Memories both glad and sad take possession of us. As it has beautified the country and fertilised the soil, so has it adorned and rendered full of lasting fruitfulness our many-sided literature. We think of the names who have immortalised it in song and story, in ballad, in drama, and novel; of its sturdy defenders in days of danger; of its sons and daughters who have carried its memory to lands far remote, whose hearts every now and then are with us in one sweet bond though leagues of ocean roll between; of the men and women who are near and dear to us on its banks, who taught our lisping tongues to sing its songs, and entranced our ears with its witching tales; of the auld schules, and the 'maisters,' and the kirks, and the hallowed acres where lie our beloved dead; of the companions who are grown men and women in life's tough conflict ; of the sweethearts we used to dream of ; of holiday haunts, and splores and pastimes when all the heart was young, and all the world a rose-strewn plain; of all the old faces and places, and stories, and memories we can conjure up at the mention of the magic name of Tweed, and never forget while life is strong and true. And it may be, when at length we feel the coming of the great Rest-bringer who comes for all, where better should we long to lay these wearied bodies than by some old-day scene on Tweed's fair river, that its gentle sigh and ripple may be the last earth-music our ears shall listen to?

IN PRAISE OF TWEED.

IN PRAISE OF TWEED.

SIR ROBERT AYTON.
1570–1638.

SIR ROBERT AYTON, descended from the original holders of the lands of Ayton, in Berwickshire, was born at his father's castle of Kinaldie, in Fifeshire, and studied first at St Leonard's College, St Andrews, where he graduated in 1588. Thereafter his studies were continued in France, from whence he addressed, in 1603, an elegant Latin panegyric to King James the Sixth on his accession to the English throne. This poem was practically the making of his fortune. From being a kind of wandering scholar-adventurer, with no definite aim in view, he blossomed into a court poet, and the confidant of no less than two of England's kings and queens. He was knighted in 1612. He was on terms of close intimacy with the leading scholars and men of letters of his time—amongst others, Thomas Hobbes and "rare Ben Jonson." Though a poet of considerable ability, his productions, for the most part in praise of his own personal friends, are penned in a spirit of conceit and fulsome flattery which cannot always be relished. He was one of the first of Scottish poets who wrote in English with any degree of force and purity. To Ayton there has been ascribed, though on very scant evidence, an original version of "Auld Lang Syne," beginning—

"Should old acquaintance be forgot,
 And never thought upon,
 The flames of love extinguished,
 And freely past and gone?

Is thy kind heart now grown so cold
 In that loving breast of thine,
That thou canst never once reflect
 On old long syne?"

He is also believed to have written the song "I do confess thou'rt smooth and fair," in which Burns, in attempting to give it a Scots garb, has succeeded so badly.

Ayton died at Whitehall Palace in 1638—a courtier to the end of his life—and was buried in the south aisle of the choir of Westminster Abbey, where the magnificent marble and copper monument erected over his grave may still be seen. His "Sonnet to the Tweed" is one of the earliest poems having this famous river for its theme. It appears to have been written on the occasion of the death of a friend by drowning.

See the Poems of Sir Robert Ayton, with Memoir by Dr Charles Rogers, London, 1871.

SONNET TO THE TWEED.

Fair, famous flood, which sometime did divide,
But now conjoins two diadems in one,
Suspend thy pace, and some more softly glide,
Since we have made thee trustman of our moan,
And since none's left but thy report alone,
To show the world our Captain's last farewell;
That corse, I know, when we are gone,
Perhaps your lord-sea will it you reveal,
And you, again, the same will not conceal;
But straight proclaim'd thro' all his bremish bounds,
Till his high tides these flowing tidings tell,
And soon will send them, with his murm'ring sounds,
To that religious place, whose stately walls
Does keep the heart, which all our hearts enthralls.

LORD YESTER.

1645–1713.

Lord Yester's lyric is described as "the key-note of Tweedside song." It is at least the earliest extant composition—with the exception of Ayton's sonnet—having for its theme the river so much belauded, and breathing the same spirit which has ever since animated the minstrelsy of the Tweed. The writer of this song was John Hay, tenth Lord Yester, third Earl, and second Marquis of Tweeddale, who took a prominent part in political affairs during the times of the Restoration, the Revolution, and the Union. He was married to the only daughter of the infamous Duke of Lauderdale. The Hays, at one period, possessed a considerable portion of the land in Peeblesshire, and in his youth Lord Yester resided at Neidpath Castle, which is most probably the scene of his lyric. Professor Veitch thus writes of Lord Yester's "Tweedside":— "In this there is true, simple feeling, simply expressed, warmed and coloured by a sense of nature around the poet—the purity of the lintwhite, the unobtrusive beauty of the goldfinch, the quiet flow of the river, happiness within reach, yet, when sought for, eluding the grasp and lost for ever. It is interesting to note that the natural objects which attracted poetic sympathy in this, the earliest remaining Tweeddale song, are the birds

Lord Yester.

of the district and the quiet of the river, unexpressed in the song, yet obviously consciously felt all through it. This appreciation of the notes of birds rather than of the colours and forms of the flowers of the field, was, I think, quite natural in the circumstances of the time. Men had been educated to a sense of sweet sounds; they had no training in painting, or any art that fitted them for the appreciation of colour or form."[1]

[1] "History and Poetry of the Scottish Border," vol. II., page 228.

TWEEDSIDE.

When Maggie and I were acquaint,
    I carried my noddle fu' hie;
Nae lintwhite in a' the gay plain,
    Nae gowdspink sae bonnie as she!
I whistled, I piped, and I sang;
    I wooed, but I cam' nae great speed;
Therefore I maun wander abroad,
    And lay my banes far frae the Tweed.

To Maggie my love I did tell,
    My tears did my passion express;
Alas! for I lo'ed her ower well,
    And the women lo'e sic a man less.
Her heart it was frozen and cauld;
    Her pride had my ruin decreed;
Therefore I maun wander abroad,
    And lay my banes far frae the Tweed.

ROBERT CRAWFORD.
1695-1732.

ROBERT CRAWFORD was the second son of Patrick Crawford, a merchant in Edinburgh, who was the third son of David Crawford, sixth laird of Drumsoy, in Renfrewshire. Patrick Crawford purchased the estate of Auchinames in 1715, which explains the statement of Burns that the son Robert was of this latter house. Of Robert Crawford's career very little is known. His elder brother Thomas was secretary to the Embassy to France under the Earl of Stair, and was afterwards appointed Envoy Extraordinary to the French Court. From this circumstance, Robert Crawford seems to have spent a part of his lifetime in France, and it is generally stated that he was drowned when returning from that country in 1732 or 1733. His best known productions are several lyrics of uncommon attractiveness, which will survive so long as Scottish song charms the ear and thrills the soul. Although a west-country man, he seems to have been wondrously wedded to Border scenery. He sang of Cowdenknowes and its "bonnie broom," of Traquair and its "birken bush," and one of the finest pastorals in the language is his "Leader Haughs and Yarrow." The finest of Crawford's songs is undoubtedly "Tweedside." "We feel that he has caught the characteristic features of the valley of the Tweed, and pictured for us a glorious spring day, in which birds sing, and the river glides brightly and gently, and the primroses spring in the woods, and the lambs bleat pathetically on the hills, and the whole air is filled with peace and love and gladness." He proves himself a thorough poet of nature, in closest sympathy with the bird creation, recognising in their sweet singing, sentiments that were only more highly developed in his own heart. The Mary referred to in "Tweedside" was Miss Mary Lilias Scott, second daughter of John Scott of Harden. A portrait of her, painted by Allan Ramsay, jun., which once adorned the walls of Hamilton Palace, shows that she must have been possessed of striking charms, and at the time when this song was written —about 1724—she must have been in brightest bloom. Sir Walter Scott styled her the *second* "Flower of Yarrow." The melody of "Tweedside" has its original—"Twid-syde"—in the Straloch MS., about 1695. At one time it was believed to have been written by David Rizzio, but for this there is not the remotest evidence. One of the songs in Gay's opera of "Polly" (1729) is set to this beautiful air.

TWEEDSIDE.

What beauties does Flora disclose!
How sweet are her smiles upon Tweed!
Yet Mary's, still sweeter than those,
Both nature and fancy exceed.

IN PRAISE OF TWEED.

No daisy, nor sweet blushing rose,
   Not all the gay flowers of the field,
Not Tweed, gliding gently through those,
   Such beauty and pleasure does yield.

The warblers are heard in the grove,
   The linnet, the lark, and the thrush;
The blackbird, and sweet cooing dove
   With music enchant every bush.

Come, let us go forth to the mead;
   Let us see how the primroses spring!
We'll lodge in some village on Tweed,
   And love while the feathered folk sing.

How does my Love pass the long day?
   Does Mary not tend a few sheep?
Do they never carelessly stray,
   While happily she lies asleep?

Should Tweed's murmurs lull her to rest,
   Kind nature indulging my bliss,
To ease the soft pains of my breast
   I'd steal an ambrosial kiss.

'T is she does the virgins excel,
   No beauty with her may compare;
Love's graces around her do dwell;
   She's fairest where thousands are fair.

Say, charmer, where do thy flocks stray?
   Oh, tell me at noon where they feed?
Shall I seek them on sweet-winding Tay,
   Or the pleasanter banks of the Tweed?

WILLIAM HAMILTON OF BANGOUR.
1704-1754.

WILLIAM HAMILTON OF BANGOUR, so named to distinguish him from William Hamilton of Gilbertfield, a contemporary poet, was born at Bangour in the parish of Uphall, Linlithgowshire. Very early in life he began to cultivate a taste for poetry, and before the age of twenty he was one of the "ingenious young gentlemen" assisting Allan Ramsay in the preparation of the *Tea-Table Miscellany* (1724). He was, we are told, the delight of the fashionable circles of his native county, possessing rank, education, and various other accomplishments, and was known as "the elegant and amiable Hamilton." In 1745 he espoused the cause of the luckless Pretender, was poet-laureate to the Jacobite army, and after the defeat at Culloden, was forced to take refuge in France and Italy. His royalist friends at home, however, successfully interceded for him. He was pardoned, and returned to Scotland in 1749. In the following year he succeeded to the paternal estates, upon the death of his elder brother. But he was not destined to enjoy them for long. His health, never robust, and shattered enough in the exile days, began to give way, and four years later he died at Lyons, where he had gone for the sake of the climate, from whence his body was conveyed home for sepulture in Holyrood Abbey. Several editions of Hamilton's works have been published. A first volume—"Poems on several occasions"— without either his name or his consent, appeared at Glasgow, in 1748, from the famous Foulis press, the preface being written by the great political economist, Adam Smith; a second edition was published at Edinburgh in 1760; but the most complete collection is that edited by James Paterson at Edinburgh, 1850. Hamilton's description of Tweedside during Autumn and Winter naturally suggests the like picture by Scott in the Introduction to Canto I. of *Marmion*. It is more than probable that Sir Walter had this in his mind when he sketched the scene, and his greater gifts as a limner are at once apparent.

But Hamilton has glorified Yarrow more than he has done Tweed. It is questionable if Border literature contains a more striking composition than his "Braes of Yarrow"—

"Busk ye, busk ye, my bonny, bonny bride"—

so full of pathos, and weirdness, and tragedy, and having running all through it the unmistaken ring of real poetry. It is the story of a Yarrow maiden whose lover has been treacherously slain by a Tweed-side laird, and who then seeks to win the love of her whom he had thus so grievously wounded. She clings to Yarrow and the old love, and all his pleadings are powerless to move her.

" Flows Yarrow sweet? as sweet, as sweet flows Tweed,
As green its grass, its gowan as yellow;
As sweet smells on its braes the birk,
The apple frae the rock as mellow."

THE SEASONS ON TWEEDSIDE.

Now Spring begins her smiling round,
Lavish to paint th' enamel'd ground;
The birds exalt their cheerful voice,
And gay on every bough rejoice;
The lovely Graces, hand in hand,
Knit in love's eternal band,
With dancing step at early dawn,
Tread lightly o'er the dewy lawn;
Where'er the youthful sisters move
They fire the soul to genial love.
Now by the river's painted side,
The swain delights his country bride,
While pleased she hears his artless vows,
Above the feathered songster's woes.
Soon will the ripen'd Summer yield
Her various gifts to every field;
The fruitful trees, a beauteous show,
With ruby-tinctur'd births shall glow;
Sweet smells, from beds of lilies born,
Perfume the breezes of the morn;
The sunny day, and dewy night,
To rural play my fair invite.
Soft on a bank of violets laid,
Cool, she enjoys the evening shade;
The sweets of Summer feast her eye—

Yet soon, soon will the Summer fly.
Attend, my lovely maid, and know
To profit by the instructive show.
Now young and blooming thou art seen,
Fresh on the stalk for ever green;
Now does the unfolded bud disclose,
Full blown to light the blushing rose:
Yet, once the sunny season past,
Think not the coz'ning scene will last.
Let not the flatterer, Hope, persuade;
Ah! must I say that it will fade?
For, see, the Summer posts away,
Sad emblem of our own decay.
Now Winter from the frozen North
Drives his stiff iron chariot forth;
His grisly hand in icy chains
Fair Tueda's silver flood constrains
Cast up thy eyes, how black and bare,
He wanders on the tops of Yair;
Behold, his footsteps dire are seen,
Confessed on every withering green;
Griev'd at the sight, when thou shalt see
A snowy wreath to clothe each tree:
Frequenting now the stream no more,
Thou fliest displeased the frozen shore;
When thou shalt miss the flowers that grew,
But late to charm thy ravished view.
Shall I, ah horrid! wilt thou say,
Be like to this some other day?
Yet, when in snow and dreary frost,
The pleasure of the field is lost,
To blazing hearths at home we run,
And fires supply the distant sun,
In gay delights our hours employ,
We do not lose, but change our joy;
Happy, abandon every care,

IN PRAISE OF TWEED.

To lead the dance, to court the fair;
To turn the page of sacred bards,
To drain the bowl, and deal the cards.
But, when the lovely white and red
From the pale ashy cheek is fled;
When wrinkles dire, and age severe,
Make beauty fly we know not where;
The fair, whom fates unkind disarm,
Have they for ever ceased to charm?
Or is there left some pleasing art
To keep secure a captive heart?
Unhappy love! might lovers say,
Beauty, thy food, does swift decay;
When once that short-lived stock is spent,
What art thy famine can prevent?
Lay virtues in with early care,
That love may live on wisdom's fare;
Tho' ecstasy with beauty flies,
Esteem is born when beauty dies;
Happy to whom the fates decree
The gift of heaven in giving thee;
Thy beauty shall his youth engage,
Thy virtues shall delight his age.

The foregoing appeared as a Song in the *Tea-Table Miscellany*, Part II.

Dr JOHN LANGHORNE.
1735-1779.

JOHN LANGHORNE, son of an English divine, was born at Kirkby-Stephen in Westmoreland. Educated for the ministry, he held various charges, and died while rector of Blagdon in Somersetshire. His *Genius and Valour: a Scottish Pastoral*, inscribed to Lord Bute "as a tribute of respect from an impartial Englishman," was written with the object of counteracting as far as possible the sarcastic statements contained in Charles Churchhill's *Prophecy of Famine*, in which he attacked Scotland and her poets—Allan Ramsay, John Home, David Malloch, and others. For this spirited defence of the sister country Langhorne was made a D.D. of Edinburgh University. "*Genius and Valour* has the usual defects of the time; it abounds in vague epithets and generalised phraseology that have no special application to the natural scenes described. Still, the poet has caught something of the echo of the places referred to and their traditions"—Veitch. The Ettrick Shepherd, in the *Queen's Wake*, thus refers not inappropriately to Langhorne:—

> "Langhorne arrived from southern dale,
> And chimed his notes on Yarrow vale;
> They would not, could not touch the heart—
> His was the modish lyre of art."

See *The Works of the English Poets*, edited by Alexander Chalmers, vol. xvi.—London, 1810.

ROBERT FERGUSSON.

HAMILTON OF BANGOUR.

ANDREW SCOTT.

WILLIAM WORDSWORTH.

From "GENIUS AND VALOUR":

A Scottish Pastoral.

Where Tweed's fair plains in liberal beauty lie,
   And Flora laughs beneath a lucid sky;
Long-winding vales where crystal waters lave,
   Where blithe birds warble, and where green woods wave,
A bright-hair'd shepherd in young beauty's bloom
   Tuned his sweet pipe beneath the yellow broom.
Free to the gale his waving ringlets lay,
And his blue eye diffused an azure day.
Light o'er his limbs a careless robe he flung,
Health raised his heart, and strength his firm nerves strung;
His native plains poetic charms inspired,
Wild scenes, where ancient Fancy oft retired!
Oft led her Faeries to the Shepherd's lay
By Yarrow's banks, or groves of Endermay.

    ✻   ✻   ✻   ✻   ✻

No more of Teviot, nor the flowery braes
Where the blithe shepherd tunes his lightsome lays;
No more of Leader's faery-haunted shore,
Of Athol's lawns, and Gledswood banks no more,
Unheeded smile my country's native charms,
Lost in the glory of her arts and arms,
These, shepherds, these demand sublimer strains
Than Clyde's clear fountains, or than Athol's plains.

    ✻   ✻   ✻   ✻   ✻

Soon wandering fearless, many a muse was seen
On the dun mountain and the wild wood green ;
Soon, to the warblings of the pastoral reed,
Started sweet echoes from the shores of Tweed.
O favoured stream where thy fair current flows,
The child of nature, gentle Thomson, rose!
Young as he wandered on thy flowery side,
With simple joy to see thy bright waves glide,
Thither in all thy native charms array'd,
From climes remote the sister "Seasons" stray'd.

MRS JOHN HUNTER.

1742-1821.

MRS JOHN HUNTER, born Anne Home, was the eldest daughter of Robert Boyne Home, a Greenlaw surgeon, connected with the Homes of Greenlaw Castle, and other families of rank. In 1771 she became the wife of John Hunter, the eminent anatomist, and from that time until her death in 1821, her life was chiefly spent in London. After her husband's death in 1793 she gave herself over to literary pursuits, leading a singularly quiet and retired life. A small volume of her poetical productions was published in 1802, and contains several compositions which have had a deserved popularity, notably amongst these the "Death-song of the Cherokee Indian," and "My mother bids me bind my hair." She was a great favourite of Hadyn, the composer, who set many of her songs to music. The song, "Farewell to Tweedside," or, as it is also entitled, "The Flowers of the Forest," originally appeared in *The Lark*, an Edinburgh journal of the year 1765, the writer being then only in her twenty-third year.

See *Minstrelsy of the Merse*, pages 85-90.

FAREWELL TO TWEEDSIDE.

Adieu, ye streams that smoothly glide
    Through mazy windings o'er the plain;
I'll in some lonely cave reside,
    And ever mourn my faithful swain.

Flower of the Forest was my love,
    Soft as the sighing summer's gale,
Gentle and constant as the dove,
    Blooming as roses in the vale.

Alas! by Tweed my love did stray,
    For me he search'd the banks around;
But, ah! the sad and fatal day
    My love, the pride of swains, was drowned!

Now droops the willow o'er the stream,
    Pale stalks his ghost in yonder grove,
Dire fancy paints him in my dream—
    Awake, I mourn my hopeless love!

JAMES HOOK.
1746–1827.

James Hook, father of the celebrated Theodore Hook, was born at Norwich, and died at Boulogne. He was the author of many operettas and songs. Of "The Banks of the Tweed," Burns says:—"This song is one of the many attempts that the English composers have made to imitate the Scottish manner, and which I shall, in these strictures, beg leave to distinguish by the appellation of "Anglo-Scottish" productions. The music is pretty good, but the verses are just above contempt."—*Reliques*, London, 1808.

If any resemblance can be traced between this melody and those of Scotland, it does not, at all events, appear to be very striking. For to what genuine Scottish air has there ever been a regular recitative prefixed? The English composer, Mr Hook, certainly never meant it should pass for a Scottish production, else he would not have displayed his name on the original title-page. This song was very popular during Mr Tenducci's residence in Scotland, and Johnson, at the request of several of his subscribers, was induced to give it an early place in his work. The greater part of the first volume of *The Museum* was engraved before Burns and Johnson became acquainted.

See Johnson's *Scots Musical Museum*, and Stenhouse's "Illustrations of the Lyric Poetry and Music of Scotland."

THE BANKS OF THE TWEED.

As on the banks of Tweed I lay reclined beneath a verdant shade
I heard a sound more sweet than pipe or flute,
Sure more enchanting was not Orpheus' lute;
While listening, and amazed, I turned my eyes—
The more I heard the greater my surprise;
I rose and followed, guided by my ear,
And in a thicket grove I saw my dear;
Unseen, unheard, she thought, thus sung the maid:

To the soft, murmuring stream I will sing of my love;
How delighted am I when abroad I can rove,
To indulge a fond passion for Jockey, my dear,
When he's absent I sigh, but how blithe when he's near.
'T is this rural amusement delights my sad heart,
Come away to my arms, Love, and never depart:
To his pipe I could sing, for he's bonnie and gay.
Did he know how I loved him, no longer he'd stay.

Neither linnet nor nightingale sung half so sweet,
And the soft, melting strain did kind echo repeat;
It so ravish'd my heart and delighted my ear,
Swift as lightning I flew to the arms of my dear.
She, surprised and detected, some moments did stand;
Like the rose was her cheek, and the lily her hand,
Which she placed on her breast, and said, Jockey, I fear
I have been too imprudent; pray, how came you here?

For to visit my ewes, and to see my lambs play,
By the banks of the Tweed and the groves I did stray;
But, my Jenny, dear Jenny, how oft have I sighed,
And have vowed endless love if you would be my bride!
To the altar of Hymen, my fair one, repair,
Where a knot of affection shall tie the fond pair;
To the pipe's sprightly notes the gay dance we will lead,
And will bless the dear grove by the banks of the Tweed.

ROBERT FERGUSSON.

1750-1774.

THE story of ROBERT FERGUSSON is surely one of the saddest on record. One cannot read it and not be moved with its depth of pathos and tragedy. Our hearts instinctively go out in strong, sterling sympathy for the ill-starred genius. Fergusson was born in Edinburgh, the third son of parents possessed of more than average intelligence. He was destined by them for the church, and in due course entered the University of St Andrews. He quickly distinguished himself as a student of unusual brilliance. Notwithstanding his immediately academic studies, poetry seems during this period to have been a chief attraction for him, and his capacity for verse-making gained him the friendship of more than one of his teachers. After four years' study he abandoned all thought of the ministry, and returned to his mother's house in Edinburgh. His father was now dead, and the family outlook by no means bright. An uncle in Aberdeenshire did not come to the aid of Robert Fergusson as had been fervently hoped. The study of medicine proved also a distasteful subject, and work in the Commissary Clerk's office, though acceptable enough, could not be said to be congenial to a lad of such promising parts. But the "daily bread" had somehow to be earned. At last there flashed on the world distinct tokens of his poetical powers. It was soon hinted that a successor to Allan Ramsay had been found, and immediately the new singer was in general demand. For a time he kept his head amid the universal laudation; but there came a change in his habits, driving him into deep excesses and the most abject self-slavery, until at last his ruin was fully wrought out. He fell into a religious melancholy, which became complete insanity after an injury to his head, received in a fall down stairs. He died in the one wretched asylum for the insane Edinburgh then possessed, and was buried in the Canongate Churchyard, where Burns, who styled Fergusson "his elder brother in the muses," erected over his grave, at his own expense, a memorial stone with the inscription:—

"No sculptur'd marble here, nor pompous lay,
No storied urn nor animated bust,
This simple stone directs pale Scotia's way
To pour her sorrows o'er her poet's dust."

Robert Fergusson kept alive the altar fire of patriotism. His imagination was coloured by ballad memories of the Border. He was the first to give Hamilton of Bangour his rightful rank as the singer of the "Braes of Yarrow," and so was among the first to celebrate that land over which lies the light of glory that shone from Sir Walter to William Wordsworth.

See *Robert Fergusson*, by Alexander B. Grosart, D.D., LL.D., in "Famous Scots" Series, 1898, and *Fergusson's Scots Poems*, W. Blackwood & Sons, 1898.

THE TWEED.

High towering on the zephyr's breezy wing,
Swift fly the Naiades from Fortha's shores,
And to the southern airy mountains bring
Their sweet enchantment and their magic powers.
    Each nymph her favourite willow takes,
    The earth with fev'rous tremor shakes,
    The stagnant lakes obey their call,
    Streams o'er the grassy pastures fall.
Tweed spreads her waters to the lucid ray,
Upon the dimpled surf the sunbeams play;
On her green banks the tuneful shepherd lies,
    Charm'd with the music of his reed,
    Amidst the wavings of the Tweed:
From sky-reflecting streams the river nymphs arise

CHORUS:

On her green banks the tuneful shepherd lies,
    Charm'd with the music of his reed,
    Amidst the wavings of the Tweed:
From sky-reflecting streams the river nymphs arise
The listening muses heard the shepherd play,
Fame with her brazen trump proclaim'd his name,
And to attend the easy graceful lay,
Pan from Arcadia to Tweeda came;
Fond of the change, along the banks he stray'd,
And sung unmindful of the Arcadian shade.

Air—"Tweedside."

I.

Attend every fanciful swain,
    Whose notes softly flow from the reed,
With harmony guide the sweet strain,
    To sing of the beauties of Tweed.

II.

Where the music of woods and of streams,
In soothing sweet melody join,
To enliven your pastoral themes,
And make human numbers divine.

CHORUS:

Ye warblers from the vocal grove,
The tender woodland strain approve,
While Tweed in smoother cadence glides,
O'er flow'ry vales in gentle tides;
And as she rolls her silver waves along,
Murmurs and sighs to quit the rural song.
Scotia's great genius, in russet clad,
From the cool sedgy bank exalts her head,
In joyful rapture she the change espies,
Sees living streams descend and groves arise.

Thames, Humber, Severn, all must yield the bay
To the pure streams of Forth, of Tweed, and Tay.

From *The Rivers of Scotland.*

THE TWEED.

The Arno and the Tiber lang
Hae run full clear in Roman sang;
But, save the reverence o' schools!
They're baith but lifeless, dowy pools,
Dought they compare wi' bonny Tweed,
As clear as ony lammer-bead?[1]

[1] An amber bead.

Or are their shores mair sweet and gay
Than Fortha's haughs or banks o' Tay.
Tho' there the herds can jink the showers
'Mang thriving vines an' myrtle bowers,
And blaw the reed to kittle strains,
While echo's tongue commends their pains,
Like ours, they canna warm the heart
Wi' simple, soft, bewitching art.
On Leader haughs an' Yarrow braes,
Arcadian herds wad tyne their lays,
To hear the mair melodious sounds
That live on our poetic grounds.
Come, Fancy! come, and let us tread
The simmer's flow'ry velvet bed,
And a' your springs delightfu' lowse
On Tweeda's banks or Cowdenknowes,
That, ta'en wi' thy enchanting sang,
Our Scottish lads may round ye thrang,
Sae pleased, they 'll never fash again
To court you on Italian plain;
Soon will they guess ye only wear
The simple garb of Nature here;
Mair comely far, and fair to sight
When in her easy cleething dight,
Than in disguise ye was before
On Tiber's, or on Arno's shore.

From *Hame Content*—a satire.

ANDREW SCOTT.
1757-1839.

ANDREW SCOTT was born at Bowden, where also Thomas Aird and James Thomson (Hawick) first beheld the light. His parents were of humble rank, and at an unusually early age he was sent out to aid in earning something for the household. He tells us that at twelve years of age he was herding in the fields. " I purchased a copy of the " Gentle Shepherd," and being charmed with the melody of the pastoral reed of Allan Ramsay, began to attempt verses in the same manner." During the second year of the American War he joined the army as a recruit and followed his regiment across the Atlantic. He served in five campaigns, and at the conclusion of the war, returned to Scotland, purchased his discharge, settled in his native parish, married, and, according to his own statement, for seventeen years abandoned the muses, assiduously applying himself to manual labour to maintain his family. But in 1805 this songless life ceased. In that year he issued a collection of his effusions, and no fewer than other four volumes followed between that date and 1826. His verse gained him the recognition of many persons of rank or literary eminence in the district—Sir Walter Scott, J. G. Lockhart, G. P. R. James, the Dukes of Buccleugh and Roxburghe, and others. Scott pursued until the close of his life the humble occupation of an agricultural labourer, and he held also the post of beadle in the parish church. He was buried at Bowden. His best poems are "Rural Content, or the Muirland Farmer," and the inimitable ballad of "Symon and Janet." In his various collections the Tweed is much besung.

MARRIAGE OF THE TWEED AND TEVIOT.

In days of yore the princely flowing Tweed
Resolved no more a single life to lead.
The fairest chief of all the watery swains
That wind their way 'mong Scotia's hills and plains,
Of all the watery nymphs toward the sea,
That from the uplands rush their mazy way,
No nymph appeared so lovely in his eyes
As the fair Teviot, and for her he sighs;
To her, his distant lover, on he flows,
Upon the north-wind murmurs all his woes;
List'ning, she hears her distant lover's wail,
And wafts her answer in the southern gale;
At length she yields—her virgin heart is won
By him, the fairest of each watery son
That, from their upland urns to wash the vales
Rush down the mountains, and the hanging dells.
And now, their mutual wishes to complete,
They set the sacred hour, and haste to meet;
Then rolls the Teviot in her crystal pride,
Anxious to meet the Tweed, a longing bride;
Each tributary stream and upland rill
Haste from their bubbling springs on many a hill;

Each naiad proud to form the nuptial train
And 'tend the bride of such a glorious swain.
Alemuir's fair daughter, from her purest lake,
To join the train is seen the Lowlands take;
Past Riddell's halls, Linthill, and Cavers' groves,
And Newhall lands, and Birsilea she roves;
Thence, hasting south, she rolls her limpid tide,
Till, passing Ancrum halls, she hails the bride.
Ettrick and Yarrow, on the bridegroom's side
In the procession, undistinguished glide;
Gala and Leader, from their urns afar
Roll with the bridegroom on his watery car;
The wildwood minstrels, as they roll along,
Pour forth their little souls in sweetest song;
From Mertoun and Makerstoun's groves they sing,
In vocal joys the listening echoes ring;
Ilk warbler lent his blithest carols there,
To grace the nuptials of so pert a pair.
The dryad nymphs, arrayed in leafy green,
To view the nuptials by the Floors convene;
Old Roxburgh's Castle's hoary genius stands
On tiptoe raised, and, with uplifted hands,
Blessed with joy the bridegroom and the bride,
Impatient now to meet. On either side
The nearing naiads, with tumultuous joy,
In louder tones their watery shells employ;
The impatient bridegroom beats his southern shore;
She beats her north, still nearing more and more;
The parting ridge between at length gives way,
And, dwindling to a point, their wills obey;
There, by the laughing banks, fair Kelso stands,
And sees with joy the parties join their hands,
As Hymen's sacred rites their nuptials grace,
Sees Teviot meet, with equal rage, her watery lord's
    embrace.

WILLIAM WORDSWORTH.
1770–1850.

To the literature of the Border country, WORDSWORTH has contributed more than most English poets. His Yarrow ballads have long been ranked among the finest productions of his pen. He had a deep affection for Scotland, and few things gave him more pleasure than to wander by Tweedside and its tributary streams. Wordsworth's first tour in Scotland, accompanied by his sister Dorothy, has been rendered quite classical through the sparkling journal of the latter. They set out from Grasmere in August 1803, and six weeks afterwards, on their way back from the Highlands, they visited Peebles and Neidpath Castle. Dorothy Wordsworth's description of this part of Tweedside is admirable. It constitutes a fitting prose poem in praise of Tweed—

" The town of Peebles is on the banks of Tweed. After breakfast, walked up the river to Neidpath Castle, about a mile and a half from the town. The castle stands upon a green hill, overlooking the Tweed, a strong, square, towered edifice, neglected and desolate, though not in ruin, the garden overgrown with grass, and the high walls that fenced it broken down. The Tweed winds between green steeps, upon which, and close to the river side, large flocks of sheep were pasturing, higher still are the grey mountains; but I need not describe the scene, for William has done it better than I could do in a sonnet which he wrote the same day; the five last lines, at least, of his poem will impart to you more of the feeling of the place than it would be possible for me to do:—

> The traveller at this day will stop and gaze
> On wrongs which Nature scarcely seems to heed;
> For sheltered places, bosoms, nooks, and bays,
> And the pure mountains and the gentle Tweed,
> And the green silent pastures yet remain.

I was spared any regret for the fallen woods when we were there, not then knowing the history of them.[1] The soft low mountains, the castle and the decayed pleasure-grounds, the scattered trees which have been left in different parts, and the road carried in a very beautiful line along the side of the hill, with the Tweed murmuring through the unfenced green pasture spotted with sheep, together composed an harmonious scene, and I wished for nothing that was not there.

When we were with Mr Scott he spoke of cheerful days he had spent in that castle, not many years ago, when it was inhabited by Professor Ferguson and his family, whom the Duke of Queensberry, its churlish owner, forced to quit it. We discovered a very fine echo within a few yards of the building."

"We had a day's journey before us along the banks

---

[1] The estate of Neidpath suffered a shameless spoliation in 1795 at the hands of the fourth Duke of Queensberry, commonly called "old Q." He sold the fine old timber which had been the pride of the neighbourhood, leaving the banks a shelterless wilderness. Wordsworth's sonnet refers to this unworthy act.

of the Tweed, a name which has been sweet to my
ears almost as far back as I can remember anything.
After the first mile or two our road was seldom far
from the river, which flowed in gentleness, though
perhaps never silent, the hills on either side high
and sometimes stony, but excellent pasturage for
sheep. In some parts the vale was wholly of this
pastoral character, in others we saw extensive
tracts of corn ground, ever spreading along the whole
hill-sides and without visible fences, which is dreary
in a flat country; but there is no dreariness on the
banks of the Tweed—the hills, whether smooth or
stony, uncultivated, or covered with ripe corn, had
the same pensive softness. Near the corn tracts
were large farm-houses, with many corn stacks;
the stacks and houses and outhouses together, I
recollect in one or two places upon the hills, at a
little distance, seemed almost as large as a small
village or hamlet. It was a clear autumnal day,
without winds, and being Sunday, the business of the
harvest was suspended, and all that we saw, and felt,
and heard, combined to excite our sensation of pensive and still pleasure.

"Passed by several old halls yet inhabited, and
others in ruins; but I have hardly a sufficiently
distinct recollection of any of them to be able to
describe them, and I now at this distance of time
regret that I did not take notes. In one very sweet
part of the vale a gate crossed the road, which was
opened by an old woman who lived in a cottage

close to it. I said to her, "You live in a very pretty place!" "Yes," she replied, "the water of Tweed is a bonnie water." The lines of the hills are flowing and beautiful, the reaches of the vale long; in some places appear the remains of a forest, in others you see as lovely a combination of forms as any traveller who goes in search of the picturesque need desire; and yet, perhaps without a single tree; or, at least, if trees there are, they shall be very few, and he shall not care whether they are there or not. The road took us through one long village, but I do not recollect any other; yet, I think we never had a mile's length before us without a house, though seldom several cottages together. The loneliness of the scattered dwellings, the more stately edifices decaying or in ruins, or, if inhabited, not in their pride and freshness, aided the general effect of the gently varying scenes, which was that of tender pensiveness; no bursting torrents when we were there, but the murmuring of the river was heard distinctly, often blended with the bleating of sheep. In one place we saw a shepherd lying in the midst of a flock upon a sunny knoll, with his face toward the sky—happy picture of a shepherd life.

" The transitions of this vale were all gentle except one, a scene of which a gentleman's house was the centre, standing low in the vale, the hills above it covered with glossy fir plantations, and the appearance of the house itself, though it could scarcely be seen, was gloomy. There was an allegorical air—

a person fond of Spenser will understand me—in this uncheerful spot, single in such a country—
"'The house was hears'd about with a black wood.' We have since heard that it was the residence of Lord Traquair, a Roman Catholic nobleman of a decayed family."[1]

Wordsworth again visited the Border country in the autumn of 1831. Sir Walter Scott was about to leave for Italy. It was a time of much sadness at Abbotsford, for it seemed probable that the great novelist might never return to his beloved haunts. He was able, however, to accompany Wordsworth and his party to Newark Castle on the Yarrow, and a memorable day seems to have been spent at this memorable spot (22nd September). "On our return in the afternoon," writes Wordsworth, "we had to cross the Tweed directly opposite Abbotsford, The wheels of our carriage grated upon the pebbles in the bed of the stream that there flows somewhat rapidly; a rich but sad light of rather a purple than a golden hue was spread over the Eildon Hills at that moment; and, thinking it probable that it might be the last time Sir Walter would cross the stream, I was not a little moved, and expressed some of my feelings in the sonnet:—

---

[1] See *Recollections of a Tour made in Scotland, A.D. 1803*. By Dorothy Wordsworth, edited by J. C. Shairp, LL.D. (Edinburgh: D. Douglas, 1874.)

See also Professor W. A. Knight's various contributions to Wordsworthian Literature.

> A trouble, not of clouds, or weeping rain,
>   Nor of the setting sun's pathetic light
>   Engendered, hangs o'er Eildon's triple height:
> Spirits of Power, assembled there, complain
>   For kindred Power departing from their sight;
> While Tweed, best pleased in chanting a blithe strain,
> Saddens his voice, again and yet again.
>   Lift np your hearts, ye Mourners ! for the might
> Of the whole world's good wishes with him goes;
>   Blessings and prayers in nobler retinue
> Than sceptred king or laurelled conqueror knows,
>   Follow this wondrous Potentate. Be true,
> Ye winds of ocean, and the midland sea,
>   Wafting your Charge to soft Parthenope!"

Just four days before, John Gibson Lockhart had penned the following farewell. He thus describes the occasion:—"On the 17th of September the old splendour of Abbotsford was, after a long interval, and for the last time, revived. Captain James Glencairn Burns, son of the poet, had come home on furlough from India, and Sir Walter invited him (with his wife, and their cicerones, Mr and Mrs M'Diarmid of Dumfries) to spend a day under his roof. The neighbouring gentry were assembled, and having his son to help him, Sir Walter did most gracefully the honours of the table. As, according to him, 'a medal struck at the time, however poor, is in one respect better than any done afterwards,' I insert some verses with which he was pleased, and which, I believe, express the sincere feelings with which every guest witnessed this his parting feast:—

LINES WRITTEN ON TWEEDSIDE.

SEPTEMBER THE 18TH, 1831.

A day I've seen whose brightness pierced the cloud
   Of pain and sorrow, both for great and small—
A night of flowing cups, and pibrochs loud,
   Once more within the Minstrel's blazoned hall.

" Upon this frozen hearth pile crackling trees;
   Let every silent clarshach find its strings;
Unfurl once more the banner to the breeze;
   No warmer welcome for the blood of kings!"

From ear to ear, from eye to glistening eye,
   Leap the glad tidings, and the glance of glee;
Perish the hopeless breast that beats not high
   At thought beneath His roof that guest to see.

What princely stranger comes?—What exiled lord
   From the far East to Scotia's strand returns?—
To stir with joy the towers of Abbotsford,
   And " wake the Minstrel's soul?"—The boy of Burns.

O, Sacred Genius! Blessing on the chains
   Wherein thy sympathy can minds entwine!
Beyond the conscious glow of kindred veins,
   A power, a spirit, and a charm are thine.

Thine offspring share them. Thou hast trod the land—
   It breathes of thee—and men, through rising tears,
Behold the image of thy manhood stand,
   More noble than a galaxy of Peers.

And He—his father's bones had quaked, I ween,
   But that with holier pride his heart-strings bound,
Than if his host had King or Kaiser been,
   And star and cross on every bosom round.

IN PRAISE OF TWEED.

High strains were poured of many a Border spear,
  While gentle fingers swept a throbbing shell;
A manly voice, in manly notes and clear,
  Of lowly love's deep bliss responded well.

The children sang the ballads of their sires;
  Serene among them sat the hoary Knight;
And, if dead Bards have ears for earthly lyres,
  The Peasant's shade was near, and drank delight.

As through the woods we took our homeward way,
  Fair shone the moon last night on Eildon Hill;
Soft rippled Tweed's broad wave beneath her ray,
  And in sweet murmurs gushed the Huntly rill.

Heaven send the guardian genius of the vale
  Health yet, and strength, and length of honoured days,
To cheer the world with many a gallant tale,
  And hear his children's children chant his lays!

Through seas unruffled may the vessel glide
  That bears her Poet far from Melrose' glen!
And may his pulse be steadfast as our pride,
  When happy breezes waft him back again! [1]

[1] See Lockhart's *Life of Scott*, Chapter LXXX.

SONNET COMPOSED AT NEIDPATH CASTLE.

Degenerate Douglas! oh, the unworthy Lord!
Whom mere despite of heart could so far please,
And love of havoc (for with such disease
Fame taxes him) that he could send forth word
To level with the dust a noble horde,
A brotherhood of venerable trees,
Leaving an ancient dome and towers like these
Beggared and outraged!—Many hearts deplored
The fate of those old trees; and oft with pain
The traveller at this day will stop and gaze
On wrongs, which Nature scarcely seems to heed;
For sheltered places, bosoms, nooks, and bays,
And the pure mountains, and the gentle Tweed,
And the green silent pastures, yet remain.

SIR WALTER SCOTT.
1771-1832.

SIR WALTER SCOTT and Tweedside are names that are shrined deep in the national heart. No man has done more for his country, and the Borderland in particular, than Scott. Though born in the Scottish capital, his ancestral associations are all with the Borders, and his own career is pre-eminently that of a Borderer in spirit and life. "His life," says Ruskin, "was, in all the joyful strength of it, spent in the valley of the Tweed. Edinburgh was his school and his office; but his home was always by Tweedside; and more perfectly so, because in three several places during the three clauses of life. The constant influences of home remain divided strictly into three eras—at Rosebank, Ashestiel, and Abbotsford. Rosebank, on the lower Tweed, gave him his close knowledge of the district of Flodden Field; and his store of foot-traveller's interest in every glen of Ettrick, Yarrow, and Liddell-water." His childhood was spent at Smailholm, just under the shadow of its grey old Tower, so fittingly styled "the outstanding sentinel of the lower valley of the Tweed." And at Kelso there began the first storing of his mind with those old legends and romances which gradually moulded him to the man he became, while here also Nature's book unfolded itself to him in a new and clearer light as he wandered amid scenes of such bewitching beauty.

"The neighbourhood of Kelso," he says in his autobiography, "the most beautiful if not the most romantic village in Scotland, is eminently calculated to awaken these ideas. It presents objects, not only grand in themselves, but venerable from their associations. The meeting of two superb rivers, the Tweed and the Teviot, both renowned in song—the ruins of an ancient Abbey—the more distant vestiges of Roxburgh Castle—the modern mansion of Fleurs, which is so situated as to combine the ideas of ancient baronial grandeur with those of modern taste—are in themselves objects of the first class; yet are so mixed, united, and melted among a thousand other beauties of a less prominent description, that they harmonise into one general picture, and please rather by unison than by concord." It was undoubtedly at Kelso that Scott's love for antiquity was awakened, and the soul of poetry first stirred within him. And those eight happy years at Ashestiel (1804-1812) were all the more happy and profitable from the memory of past days by the banks of the Tweed. For Scott's happiest time was certainly at Ashestiel, and it has been said that had he been able to purchase this property, Abbotsford would never have arisen from the swamps of "Cartley Hole." At Ashestiel his fame as a poet was established and 'before his lease expired he had wreathed with poesy the whole surrounding district, making Ashestiel a more interesting place to students of his poems than any of his other residences.'"

"There it stands," writes Wilson in his *Anglimania*, "half-embowered, above the bowers that here, more than anywhere else, to our eyes do indeed beautify the Tweed. It holds in kind command all the banks and braes about, with their single trees dropped here and there in 'Nature's careless haste,' and rich with many a stately grove overhanging the river's gleam, or within hearing of its murmurs. But the green hills behind the house are now sloping away up to the far mists that seem to be hiding mountains; and the scene, though sweet, is not without grandeur. Of yore it was the home of— THE MAGICIAN. Here we first saw—Walter Scott. 'Twas in the summer he was writing Marmion. In the evening he chanted from the quarto sheets the two first cantos, with look, voice, and action appropriate to the spirit-stirring poetry of war."

About the end of May, 1812, Scott and his family removed to Abbotsford, which, originally a small and mean farm, he had purchased the previous year from the Rev. Dr Douglas of Galashiels. Then began the building of his 'romance in stone and lime,' and the working out of his life's ambition.

Bit by bit, Sir Walter added to his Tweedside domain, so that by 1832 it had become the foremost house on all the noble river, the attraction alike of king and commoner, of all who could prize the intellectual supremacy of its worthy lord. And here on that memorable autumn afternoon the 'mighty minstrel' breathed his last. "It was a beautiful day, so warm that every window was wide open, and so perfectly still that the sound of all others most delicious to his ear—the gentle ripple of the Tweed over its pebbles—was distinctly audible as we knelt around the bed and his eldest son kissed and closed his eyes." By Tweedside, too, he was borne to the last resting-place, and many hearts were touched with that final crossing of the Tweed at Leaderfoot; and, when at length they laid him among the tombs of his ancestors in Dryburgh's ruined pile, it was felt that no more appropriate place of sepulture could have been for one who had raised himself to be the central glory of Tweedside.

NOVEMBER ON TWEEDSIDE.

"November's sky is chill and drear,
November's leaf is red and sere:
Late, gazing down the steepy linn
That hems our little garden in,
Low in its dark and narrow glen
You scarce the rivulet might ken,
So thick the tangled greenwood grew,
So feeble trilled the streamlet through;
Now, murmuring hoarse, and frequent seen
Through bush and briar, no longer green,
An angry brook, it sweeps the glade,

IN PRAISE OF TWEED.

Brawls over rock and wild cascade,
And foaming brown, with doubled speed,
Hurries its waters to the Tweed.
No longer Autumn's glowing red
Upon our Forest hills is shed:
No more, beneath the evening beam,
Fair Tweed reflects their purple gleam;
Away hath passed the heather-bell
That bloomed so rich on Neidpath Fell;
Sallow his brow, and russet-bare
Are now the sister-heights of Yair.
The sheep, before the pinching heaven,
To sheltered dale and down are driven,
Where yet some faded herbage pines,
And yet a watery sunbeam shines;
In meek despondency they eye
The withered sward and wintry sky,
And, far beneath their summer hill,
Stray sadly by Glenkinnon's rill;
The shepherd shifts his mantle's fold,
And wraps him closer from the cold;
His dogs no merry circles wheel,
But, shivering, follow at his heel;
A cowering glance they often cast,
As deeper moans the gathering blast.
My imps, though hardy, bold, and wild
As best befits the mountain child,
Feel the sad influence of the hour,
And wail the daisy's vanished flower;
Their summer gambols tell, and mourn,
And anxious ask—Will Spring return,
And birds and lambs again be gay,
And blossoms clothe the hawthorn spray?"

*   *   *   *   *

" The vision of enchantment 's passed :
Like frostwork in the morning ray,
The fancied fabric melts away ;
Each Gothic arch, memorial-stone,
And long, dim, lofty aisle, are gone ;
And, lingering lost, deception dear,
The choir's high sounds die on my ear,
Now slow return the lonely down,
The silent pastures, bleak and brown,
The farm begirt with copsewood wild,
The gambols of each frolic child
Mixing their shrill cries with the tone
Of Tweed's dark waters rushing on."

From Introduction to *Marmion*, Canto I. ; written at Ashestiel

NOVEMBER ON TWEEDSIDE (AND ON YARROW).

Even now it scarcely seems a day,
Since first I tuned this idle lay ;
A task so often thrown aside,
When leisure graver cares denied,
That now, November's dreary gale,
Whose voice inspired my opening tale,
That same November gale once more
Whirls the dry leaves on Yarrow shore.
Their vex'd boughs streaming to the sky,
Once more our naked birches sigh,
And Blackhouse heights, and Ettrick Pen,
Have donn'd their wintry shrouds again ;
And mountain dark, and flooded mead,
Bid us forsake the banks of Tweed.
Earlier than wont, along the sky,
Mixed with the rack, the snow-mists fly ;

The shepherd, who, in summer sun,
Had something of our envy won,
As thou with pencil, I with pen,
The features traced of hill and glen—
He who, outstretch'd the livelong day,
At ease among the heath-flowers lay,
View'd the light clouds with vacant look,
Or slumber'd o'er his tatter'd book,
Or idly busied him to guide
His angle o'er the lessen'd tide.
At midnight now, the snowy plain
Finds sterner labour for the swain.
When red hath set the beamless sun,
Through heavy vapours dark and dun;
When the tired ploughman, dry and warm,
Hears, half-asleep, the rising storm
Hurling the hail, and sleeted rain,
Against the casement's tinkling pane;
The sound that drives wild-deer, and fox,
To shelter in the brake and rocks,
Are warnings which the shepherd ask
To dismal and to dangerous task.
Oft he looks forth, and hopes, in vain,
The blast may sink in mellowing rain;
Till, dark above, and white below,
Decided drives the flaky snow,
And forth the hardy swain must go.
Long, with dejected look and whine,
To leave the hearth his dogs repine;
Whistling and cheering them to aid,
Around his back he wreathes the plaid:
His flock he gathers, and he guides
To open downs, and mountain-sides,
Where, fiercest though the tempest blow,
Least deeply lies the drift below.
The blast, that whistles o'er the fells,

Stiffens his locks to icicles;
Oft he looks back, while streaming far,
His cottage window seems a star—
Loses its feeble gleam—and then
Turns patient to the blast again,
And, facing to the tempest's sweep,
Drives through the gloom his lagging sheep.
If fails his heart, if his limbs fail,
Benumbing death is in the gale;
His paths, his landmarks, all unknown,
Close to the hut no more his own,
Close to the aid he sought in vain,
The morn may find the stiffened swain;
The widow sees, at dawning pale,
His orphans raise their feeble wail;
And, close beside him, in the snow,
Poor Yarrow, partner of their woe,
Couches upon his master's breast,
And licks his cheek to break his rest.
Who envies now the shepherd's lot,
His healthy fare, his rural cot,
His summer couch by greenwood tree,
His rustic kirn's loud revelry,
His native hill-notes turned on high,
To Marion of the blithesome eye;
His crook, his scrip, his oaten seed,
And all Arcadia's golden creed?

From Introduction to *Marmion*, Canto IV.; written at Ashestiel.

DECEMBER ON TWEEDSIDE.

When dark December glooms the day,
And takes our Autumn joys away;
When short and scant the sunbeam throws

Upon the weary waste of snows
A cold and profitless regard,
Like patron on a needy bard;
When silvan occupation's done,
And o'er the chimney rests the gun,
And hang, in idle trophy, near,
The game-pouch, fishing-rod, and spear
When wiry terrier, rough and grim,
And greyhound, with his length of limb,
And pointer, now employ'd no more,
Cumber our parlour's narrow floor;
When in his stall the impatient steed
Is long condemned to rest and feed;
When from our snow-encircled home,
Scarce cares the hardiest step to roam,
Since path is none, save that to bring
The needful water from the spring;
When wrinkled news-page, thrice conn'd o'er,
Beguiles the dreary hour no more,
And darkling politician, cross'd,
Inveighs against the lingering post,
And answering housewife sore complains
Of carriers' snow-impeded wains;
When such the country cheer, I come,
Well pleased, to seek our city home;
For converse, and for books, to change
The Forest's melancholy range,
And welcome, with renewed delight,
The busy day and social night.

From Introduction to *Marmion*, Canto V. written at Edinburgh.

CHRISTMAS ON TWEEDSIDE.

Heap on more wood!—the wind is chill;
But, let it whistle as it will,

We'll keep our Christmas merry still.
Each age has deem'd the new-born year
The fittest time for festal cheer.

*   *   *   *   *

And well our Christian sires of old
Loved when the year its course had roll'd,
And brought blithe Christmas back again,
With all his hospitable train;
Domestic and religious rite
Gave honour to the holy night;
On Christmas eve the bells were rung;
On Christmas eve the mass was sung;
That only night in all the year,
Saw the stoled priest the chalice rear.
The damsel donn'd her kirtle sheen;
The hall was dressed with holly green;
Forth to the wood did merry-men go,
To gather in the mistletoe;
Then open'd wide the baron's hall,
To vassal, tenant, serf, and all;
Power laid his rod of rule aside,
And Ceremony doffed his pride;
The heir, with roses in his shoes,
That night might village partner choose;
The lord, underogating, share
The vulgar game of " post and pair."
All hailed with uncontroll'd delight,
And general voice, the happy night,
That to the cottage, as the crown
Brought tidings of salvation down.
The fire, with well-dried logs supplied,
Went roaring up the chimney wide;
The huge hall-table's oaken face,
Scrubb'd till it shone, the day to grace,
Bore then upon its massive board

No mark to part the squire and lord;
Then was brought in the lusty brawn,
By old blue-coated serving-man;
Then the grim boar's head frown'd on high,
Crested with bays and rosemary,
Well can the green-garbed ranger tell,
How, when, and where the monster fell;
What dogs before his death he tore,
And all the baiting of the boar.
The wassel round, in good brown bowls,
Garnished with ribbons, blithely trowls,
There the huge sirloin reeked; hard by
Plum-porridge stood, and Christmas pie;
Nor failed old Scotland to produce,
At each high tide, her savoury goose,
Then came the merry maskers in,
And carols roared with blithesome din;
If unmelodious was the song,
It was a hearty note, and strong.
Who lists may in their mumming see
Traces of ancient mystery;
White shirts supplied the masquerade,
And smutted cheeks the visors made;
But, O! what maskers, richly dight,
Can boast of bosoms half so light!
England was merry England, when
Old Christmas brought her sports again.
'T was Christmas broach'd the mightiest ale;
'T was Christmas told the merriest tale;
A Christmas gambol oft could cheer
The poor man's heart through half the year.
Still linger, in our northern clime,
Some remnants of the good old time;
And still, within our valleys here,
We hold the kindred title dear,
Even when, perchance, its far-fetched claim

IN PRAISE OF TWEED. 51

To Southron ear sounds empty name;
For course of blood, our proverbs deem,
Is warmer than the mountain-stream.
And thus, my Christmas still I hold,
Where my great-grandsire came of old,
With amber beard, and flaxen hair,
And reverend apostolic air—
The feast and holy-tide to share,
And mix sobriety with wine,
And honest mirth with thoughts divine;
Small thought was his, in after time,
E'er to be hitched into a rhyme.
The simple sire could only boast
That he was loyal to his cost;
The banish'd race of kings revered,
And lost his land—but kept his beard.
In these dear halls, where welcome kind,
Is with fair liberty combined;
Where cordial friendship gives the hand,
And flies constraint the magic wand
Of the fair dame that rules the land.
Little we heed the tempest drear,
While music, mirth, and social cheer,
Speed on their wings the passing year.
And Mertoun's halls are fair e'en now,
When not a leaf is on the bough,
Tweed loves them well, and turns again,
As loath to leave the sweet domain,
And holds his mirror to her face,
And clips her with a close embrace—
Gladly as he, we seek the dome,
And as reluctant turn us home.

From Introduction to *Marmion*, Canto VI., written at Mertoun House.

JOHN LEYDEN.

1775-1811.

JOHN LEYDEN, sometimes called JOHN CASPAR LEYDEN, third in the great triumvirate of Border literature — Scott, Hogg, Leyden — was born at Denholm, one of the loveliest villages in Teviotdale. Educated for a few years at the district schools, he then entered the University of Edinburgh, where he had a brilliant career. He was a hard-working student. His *forte* was classics. His ruling passion was to possess in a very real sense the gift of tongues; and he succeeded. His after career is abundant proof of this. He became master of no fewer than a score of languages, and was acquainted more or less with as many dialects. Destined for the ministry of the Scottish Church he was licensed as a preacher in 1798. But he signally failed in this sphere, and betook himself to literature. He became a book-producer, a contributor to many journals and collections of poetry. All his life he had been specially attracted to the legendary lore of his country, and had been known to tramp forty miles for an old ballad, which it was believed only one man could repeat in full. He was Scott's most valued coadjutor in the preparation of the "Border Minstrelsy." He assisted "Monk" Lewis in his "Tales of Wonder." He managed for a time the "Scots Magazine." He edited the "Complaint of

JOHN LEYDEN

Scotland," and a collection of "Scottish Descriptive Poems." He wrote on African discovery (which continent he was eager to explore); on Scottish literary antiquities; on fairy superstition; on the Ossian controversy; and on his favourite theme of philology. By-and-bye he took to the study of medicine, and graduated M.D. of St Andrews. Accepting of an appointment as surgeon in the East India Company's service at Madras, he sailed for India, and rapidly rose in rank while he busied himself with the most useful undertakings. To the irreparable loss of his country he died at the early age of thirty-six, just when the brightest prospects were opening up before him. John Leyden is perhaps better known to most as the poet of his native vale. As such he lives in the affection of all Borderers. Exquisitely sweet and tender is his "Scenes of Infancy." No poem will better preserve and shrine for all time those places, ever dear and long-remembered in the patriot mind, that lie so divinely beautiful in the heart of the Borderland.

For many additional particulars of his Indian career, not noticed in the Biographical Sketches of Leyden, see D. C. Boulger's Life of Sir Stamford Raffles, 1898. London: Horace Marshall & Sons.

THE TWEED AT KELSO.

Teviot, farewell! for now thy silver tide
Commix'd with Tweed's pellucid stream shall glide,
But all thy green and pastoral beauties fail
To match the softness of thy parting vale.
Bosom'd in woods, where mighty rivers run,
Kelso's fair vale expands before the sun;
Its rising downs in vernal beauty swell,
And, fring'd with hazel, winds each flowery dell;
Green spangled plains to dimpling lawns succeed,
And Tempé rises on the banks of Tweed.
Blue o'er the river Kelso's shadow lies;
And copse-clad isles amid the waters rise;
Where Tweed her silent way majestic holds,
Float the thin gales in more transparent folds,
New powers of vision on the eye descend,
As distant mountains from their bases bend,
Lean forward from their seats, to court the view,
While melt their soften'd tints in vivid blue;
But fairer still, at midnight's shadowy reign,
When liquid silver floods the moonlight plain,
And lawns, and fields, and woods of varying hue,
Drink the wan lustre, and the pearly dew;
While the still landscape, more than noontide bright,
Glistens with mellow tints of fairy light.

From *Scenes of Infancy*, Part III.

JOHN WILSON.

1785-1854.

"CHRISTOPHER NORTH" was a native of Paisley, the eldest son of a rich, self-made manufacturer of gauze; his mother, Margaret Sym, being a descendant of the great Marquis of Montrose. Educated first at the Manse of Mearns, a wild moorland parish in Renfrewshire, he afterwards studied at Glasgow University, where he distinguished himself in carrying off a number of prizes, and by a manifest gift of verse-making. His father died in 1797, leaving him a fortune of £50,000. In 1803 he entered Magdalen College, Oxford, as a gentleman-commoner, and during his four years' residence, was a notable figure, alike for his intellectual qualities and his powers as an athlete. In 1807 he purchased the small but charming estate of Elleray, overlooking Lake Windermere, and settled down amid the congenial companionship of such men as Wordsworth, Southey, Coleridge, De Quincey, and others. In 1811 he married, and began in earnest to devote himself to literary pursuits. But in 1815 a terrible blow befel him in the loss of his whole patrimony, through the unjust stewardship of an uncle, in whom he had placed implicit confidence. Like Scott, he had now to retrieve his shattered fortunes, and commenced to study for the Scottish Bar; but this kind of life did not suit him, and he speedily abandoned it in favour of literary work which cropped up through the establishment of *Blackwood's Magazine*; and by-and-bye he became practically the editor of that always popular journal. In 1820 he was elected to the Moral Philosophy Chair in Edinburgh University, which he held until his death in April, 1854. Professor Wilson caught up, as few men have done, the true spirit of the Borders. He was at home in every nook and crannie of the Border country, and nothing afforded him greater delight than a piscatorial excursion to Tweedside. It was not only the sport which enticed him thither, but the romantic associations of the whole district had a strong fascination for him; and his heart had learned to knit itself in ties of leal and lasting friendship to the honest, kindly men of its hills and glens. His description of the Tweed near its source is highly characteristic, and there are other passages in the *Noctes* and elsewhere which show how much Wilson owed to the Borders of Scotland for that *perfervidum ingenium Scotorum* which made him one of the most beloved figures in our social and literary life. His works were edited by his son-in-law, Professor Ferrier (12 vols., 1855-58).

See the *Memoir* by his daughter, Mrs Gordon, 1862; and *The Blackwood Group*, by Sir George Douglas (Famous Scots Series, 1897).

THE TWEED AT TWEEDSMUIR.

You observe we have a pannier on our shoulder, and a fishing-rod in its numerous pieces, not unlike the Roman fasces. You must know that we are on our way to the Crook Inn in Tweedsmuir. Ostensibly, we are going to angle; but the truth is, that that is almost a pretence. An elderly gentleman, ever since Dr Johnson's verses, looks absurd in his hat and wig by the side of a murmuring stream; so we have mounted a foraging-cap and let our few silver hairs take their chance in this genial weather. With our angle in our hand, we shall be able to dauner down the streams without awakening suspicions of sanity or suicide in the minds of the shepherds; and not improbably we may kill, without intending it, a glowing, golden, starry-sided Prince of the Pool, who has reigned a lustrum over a populous empire of trouts and minnows.

"The Tweed, the Tweed, be blessings on the Tweed!" Bagmen, behold the Tweed! It issues from the blue mist of yonder mountain, *Scotticè* Erickstane. The very wheels of the mail—the axle himself, is loth to disturb the liquid murmur. That sound—call it a noise, for it is brawling jocundly—is from some scores of tiny waterfalls, up among the braes, all joining, like children's voices the leader of an anthem, the clear, strong tenor of the Tweed. A blind man, with a musical ear, might almost be said to see the river. Yonder it is—one bright gleam, like that of a little tarn; but a cloud has been passing, and the gleam disappearing, there you behold at once a quarter of a mile of stream, pool, and shallow—cattle grazing on the holms, sheep dotting the hills—over yonder grove, too distant to be heard, the circling flight of rooks, and tending thitherward, a pair of herons, seemingly unmindful of this lower world, yet both crammed as full as they can fly with fishes from the moor-lochs—more easily caught, perhaps, by the silent watchers than the stream trouts; or, rather, do not herons prefer such angling, because Gameshope is a lonesome loch, and they have it all to themselves—their own silent preserve?

But lo! the Crook Inn, and we must say, "farewell" to guard and bagmen. . . . . A few gulps of Tweedsmuir air have made us quite a young elderly gentleman. . . . . A single blockhead, or even a batch of blockheads, would be miserable at the Crook Inn. There is no stir on the road to stare at—two or three chaises, perhaps, at the utmost, during a whole day at this season; and now and then a farmer, jogging by with—it may be—his wife behind him on a pillion. Nothing to look at but green hills—a few flat potato-fields, covered with pyramids of dung, and a river—name by blockhead unknown and unasked—with a din more wearisome and monotonous than a hurdy-gurdy. But, reader, neither you nor we are a blockhead; so, happy could we be together, or apart, with the 'Crook in our lot,' all a summer's day; for who, with a heart and a soul tolerably at ease within him, could fail to be happy, hearing, as we do now, the voice of the Tweed, singing his pensive twilight song to the few faint stars that have become visible in heaven? Let us dauner away, then, along to the banks of the Tweed, and, if the dews be not too heavy, lie down, like one of the other resting and ruminating creatures, on the close-nibbled braes. Nothing is farther from our thoughts than the wish to be poetical; yet who can escape being so Scott-free when walking alone by Tweedside under one of the most beautiful of April night-skies? There is no silence except where there is sound. Silence is an active power when overcoming sound, as it does when the continual calm contest is carrying on in the solitude of the hills. The louder the voice of the stream, the deeper the sleep of the air! Nothing can awaken it till morning melt the dream. Should a distant dog bark, hunting by himself on the hill, or disturbed, perhaps, by the foot of some strange shepherd, visiting his Peggy when the household are asleep, how the faint, far-off echoes give power to the brooding calm! Wearied labour is everywhere thankfully at rest; and love, and joy, and youth alone are wakeful. No wonder that poets glorified the glimpses of the moon, and, long before science was born, named, and arranged, and localised the stars. So sayeth Kit North, beadsman of Tweedside.

It would puzzle us to tell why the Tweed is to us the dearest of all the streams of Scotland. Our father's house stood not on its banks, nor on them played our infancy nor our boyhood. Perhaps we are thus able to love it with that unregretful and impassionate affection, without which the human spirit cannot find happiness in nature. Oh! there are places on this earth that we shudder to revisit even in a waking dream, beneath the meridian sunshine. They are haunted by images too beautiful to be endured, and the pangs are dismal that clutch the heart, when approaching their bewildering boundaries! for there it was that we roamed in the glorious novelty of nature, when we were innocent and uncorrupted. There it was that we lived in a world without shadows, almost without tears; and, after grief and guilt have made visitations to the soul, she looks back in agony to those blissful regions of time and space, when she lived in Paradise. Nor are any flaming swords in the hands of cherubim needed to guard the gates, through which she dares not, if flung wide open, now to enter, in the abasement of her despair. Therefore she takes refuge in the dim and obscure light of common day, and seeks scenery not so mournfully haunted by the ghosts of thoughts that glorified the dawn of her prime.

Who has not felt something of this, although the forms round which the memory of his boyhood clings may, in his particular case, be different? But, reader, if thy early footsteps were free and unconfined over the beautiful bosom of the rejoicing earth, thou wilt understand the passion that the dream of some one solitary spot may inspire, rising suddenly up from oblivion in all its primeval loveliness, and making a silent appeal to thy troubled heart, in behalf of innocence evanished long ago, and for ever! From the image of such spots you start away, half in love, half in fear, as from the visionary spectre of some dear friend dead and buried, far beyond seas in a foreign country, Such power as this may there be in the little moorland rill, oozing from the birchen brae—in some one of its fairy pools, that, in your lonely angling days, seemed to you more especially delightful, as it swept sparkling and singing through the verdant wilderness—in some one deep streamless dell among a hundred, too insignificant to have received any name from the shepherds, but first discovered and enjoyed by you, when the soul within you was bright with the stirred fire of young existence—in some sheltered, retired nook, whither all the vernal hill-flowers had seemed to flock, both for shadow and sunshine, in some greenest glade, far within the wood's heart, on which you had lain listening to the cushat crooning in his yew grove—ay, in one and all of such places, and a thousand more, you feel that a power for ever dwells omnipotent over your spirit, adorned, expanded, strengthened, although it may now be, with knowledge and science—a power extinguishing all present objects, and all their accompanying thoughts and emotions, in the inexpressibly pensive light of those blissful days, when time and space were both bounded to a point by the perfect joy of the soul that existed in that NOW, happier than any angel in heaven."

"Oh! we feel that we were deceiving ourselves when we said that our old age was not subject to the Anglimania. We would not give up the prospect of this day's sport to be the Right Honourable Frederick Robinson, Chancellor of the Exchequer! Nothing drumly about the sweet Tweed this morning—no pool the colour of porter with barmy foam—but the deeps a black blue, and the shallows a dark green, covered with foam-bells that break beneath the breeze's warm-breathing from the South-South-West, the angler's darling airt. Yes—

"O a' the airts the wind can blaw,
He dearly lo'es the West!"

From Essay on *Streams*—April, 1826.

JOHN ALEXANDER PRINGLE.

1792–1839.

JOHN ALEXANDER PRINGLE, second son of Alexander Pringle of Yair, was born at Yair, April 17, 1792. His life was spent chiefly in the Bengal Civil Service. He was a man of general literary tastes, and wrote some pleasing poetry, a selection of which was issued for private circulation in 1841— "Select Remains of John Alexander Pringle, Yr. of Yair," London: Harrison & Co. The volume is now extremely rare. He died at Castledykes, near Dumfries, January 3, 1839, and was buried in the Yair family burying-place in Melrose Abbey.

See *Memoir* by Sir Andrew Halliday.

A DREAM OF TWEEDSIDE.

I like your castle in the air,
But, Maggy, lass, I'm far frae Yair,
Wi' pouches toom, it's unco sair
    To toddle hame;
But, though I'm here, my thoughts are there,
    And that's the same.

I 'm surely dazed, I think I 'm there,
I canna sing, I dinna care,
I hum the "Bush aboon Traquair,"
    And doon the brae,
Ayont Rowlees, a keek o' Yair
    I dream I hae.

Whist!—Why glow'd my cheek as o'er yon knowe
    My weary footsteps bore me?
Why lap my heart as it would part
    And win the glen afore me?
I saw frae there my hame ance mair;
    Oh, how the sight did cheer me!
Ilk weel ken't glen, the braes o' Tweed
    Wi' lang lost joys were near me.
Ye rich, wha fortune find at hame,
    An' ilka pleasure catch at,
A wanderer puir ae joy could name
    Your wealth could never match that.
Your warmest thought can fancy nought
    I felt as hame grew nearer;
Ance mair to see the braes o' Tweed—
    What braes to me are dearer?
Ay, Mag, I mind, but ne'er can tell
    My joy when first I saw them;
The rainbow's tints aboon yon hill!
    What painter e'er could draw them?
Though Fortune's wheel should crush me still,
    Though Care's rough thorns should tear me;
The day I saw the braes o' Tweed
    I 'll mind—the thought will cheer me.

From *Select Remains*.

Professor John Wilson.

David Macbeth Moir.

Yours ever truly
Henry Scott Riddell

William Air Foster.

DAVID MACBETH MOIR ("DELTA").

1798-1851.

DAVID MACBETH MOIR, M.D., a distinguished writer under the pseudonym of "Delta," was born at Musselburgh. He graduated in medicine at Edinburgh University in 1817, and practised with much success as a physician in his native town until his death on 6th July, 1851. He wrote the famous Scottish story of *Mansie Wauch*, certainly one of the best productions of the Scottish school of fiction. His poetry, though not extensive, has taken a high rank with readers. *Casa Wappy*, written on the death of a favourite child, is one of the most touching and perfectly finished elegies in the language. "Delta" made a tour of the Border country in 1829, visiting most of the storied scenes on the Tweed. The centenary of his birth was celebrated with due honour at Musselburgh on January 5, 1898.

See *Memoir* by Thomas Aird, prefixed to collected edition of his poems (1852), and *Domestic Verses* (centenary edition).—Blackwood, Edinburgh.

IN PRAISE OF TWEED.

DRYBURGH ABBEY.

Beneath, Tweed murmured 'mid the forests green;
  And through thy beech-tree and laburnum boughs,
  A solemn ruin, lovely in repose,
Dryburgh! thine ivy'd walls were greyly seen;
  Thy court is now a garden, where the flowers
Expand in silent beauty, and the bird,
Flitting from arch to arch, alone is heard
  To cheer with song the melancholy bowers.
Yet did a solemn pleasure fill the soul,
  As through thy shadowy cloistral cells we trode,
  To think, poor pile! that once thou wert the abode
Of men, who could to solitude control
  Their hopes—yea! from Ambition's pathways stole,
  To give their whole lives blamelessly to God!

From *Sonnets on the Scenery of the Tweed.*

HENRY SCOTT RIDDELL.

1798-1870.

HENRY SCOTT RIDDELL, one of the lealest sons the Border country ever knew, whose life was unhappily marred in the midst of its usefulness, was born at Sorbie, in the valley of Ewes, near Langholm. Like his greater brother - bard of Ettrick, he came of a race of shepherds, and for a time also followed that vocation. Settling in the Border country, as more distinctly understood, where Yarrow and Ettrick and Tweed are the names that knit us to their silver flow, young Riddell found himself being resistlessly drawn to the study of the old Border life and its fascinating record of song and story. He shepherded at Deloraine, among the green hills of Yarrow, and at Todrig, near Hawick, where he forgathered with William Knox of Lilliesleaf, the poet of the Lanely Hearth, whose friendship and influence tended considerably to mould Riddell's poetical tastes. Next we find him at Biggar, in the upper ward of Lanarkshire, preparing for college life and working hard at classes under a skilled and kindly teacher. Then he appears as a student at the University of Edinburgh, attracting the attention of Professor Dunbar by his clever translations, and winning the friendship of Christopher North, whose large, manly heart was always open to such a type of student as Riddell must have been. By-and-bye we find him settled in the ministry (though not ordained) at the preaching station of Teviothead, and nobly fulfilling his pastoral duties amid all the drawbacks of a manseless minister, being resident as far distant as nine miles from his little flock. His ministry at Teviothead was much appreciated by all his parishioners, and here in 1841 the blow fell which practically snapped the pastoral tie between him and them. There were many manifestations of sorrow and generous sympathy. After being an inmate for some time in the Crichton Royal Institution at Dumfries, Riddell returned to Teviothead completely and permanently cured, but it was deemed advisable that he should not resume his duties as minister. He continued to reside in the cottage that had been built for him by the Duke of Buccleugh, and died there in 1870. Henry Scott Riddell was a prolific versifier, and many of his songs have reached a wide popularity. While it cannot be claimed for him that he takes rank with the great singers of the country, he has, nevertheless, a firm and an assured place in the affections of the Scottish people all over the world. So long as the strong feelings of patriotism and the gentler passions of the human breast are uppermost, it is unlikely that we shall forget such inspiring sentiments as "Scotland Yet," "Scotia's Thistle," "Oor Ain Folk," or "The Wild Glen sae Green." Henry Scott Riddell spent his life amongst the peasantry.

For them he wrote most of his songs, and though these are now the possession of all classes, by none is his memory more lovingly cherished than by the warm-hearted and sympathetic people of the Scottish Borders. "Bonnie Tweedside" is founded on an old song and tune to which Allan Ramsay also wrote some verses, which may be found among his "Scots Songs."

See *Memoirs of H. S. Riddell*, by James Brydon, M.D., Hawick, prefixed to Poetical Works; 2 vols. Glasgow, 1871.
See also *Scotland Yet* and other verses, by H. S. Riddell; edited, with Memoir, by W. S. Crockett. Hawick, 1898. (Centenary Edition.)

BONNIE TWEEDSIDE.

We'll a' away to bonnie Tweedside,
   And see my dearie come through;
We'll a' away to bonnie Tweedside,
   And see my dearie come through,
For the light o' the morn shall cease to return,
   Ere I forget my vow;
And we'll a' away to bonnie Tweedside,
   And see my dearie come through:
Her locks are like the links o' gowd,
   That wave o'er her snaw-white broo;
Her lip is pure as the hawthorn bud,
   When wet wi' the morning dew;
Her bosom is white as the heaving clud,
   And her heart is warm and true;
And we'll a' away to bonnie Tweedside,
   And see my dearie come through.

IN PRAISE OF TWEED.

'T is sweet to see, on bonnie Tweedside,
    The spring a' its charms renew,
And hear, as sung frae the woodlands wide,
    The sangs o' our land sae true;
And sweet to stray, through the summer day,
    In the glens where the forests grew,
But sweeter to ride to bonnie Tweedside,
    And welcome ane's dearie through.
The bower is blinking aboon the brae,
    Where the days o' childhood flew;
When hope was bright and the heart was light,
    And the cares o' life were few;
But the day has come that is mair to some
    Than a' that their childhood knew,
And we'll a' away to bonnie Tweedside,
    And welcome my dearie through.

The flowers shall smile on bonnie Tweedside,
    To see my dearie come through,
As they lift their blooms in beauteous pride,
    'Mang the grass and the balmy dew—
The laverocks spring on their airy wing,
    And the lambs their play renew,
And we'll a' away to bonnie Tweedside,
    And welcome my dearie through.
A' busket braw are the grit and the sma',
    And blithely the path pursue,
And crowd to see the lovely and free,
    And the maid o' the heart sae true;
In a busy mood, the wise and the good
    Speak a' o' her merit due,
And we'll a' be blessed wi' cheer o' the best,
    If ance my dearie were through.

WILLIAM AIR FOSTER.

1801–1862.

WILLIAM AIR FOSTER, born at Coldstream in 1801, was by trade a shoemaker, first in his native town, and afterwards in Glasgow, where he died in 1862. He was an enthusiastic Border sportsman, a distinguished champion in all games, excelling especially in archery, in which it is stated he had no rival at the time. His best songs are those animated by the thrilling excitements of this kind of life, and are characterised by splendid descriptive power and life-like touches. He was an attached friend of the Ettrick Shepherd. Though a prolific versifier, he published very little, his chief contributions being made to "Whistle Binkie" and the "Book of Scottish Song."

THE BONNIE TWEED FOR ME.

Air—"YON BURNSIDE."

The hunter's e'e grows bright as the fox frae covert steals,
The fowler lo'es the gun, wi' the pointer at his heels,
But, o' a' the sports I ken that can stir the heart wi' glee,
The troutin' stream, the fishin' gad, the bonnie Tweed for me.

IN PRAISE OF TWEED.

Wi' the gowan at the waterside, the primrose on the brae,
When sheets o' snawy blossom cleed the cherry and the slae,
When sun and wind are wooin' baith the leaflet on the tree,
Then the troutin' stream, the fishin' gad, the bonnie Tweed for me.

When the fresh green sward is yieldin' wi' a spring aneath the fit,
And swallows thrang on eager wing out o'er the waters flit,
While the joyous laverocks, toorin' high, shoor out their concert free,—
Then the troutin' stream, the fishin' gad, the bonnie Tweed for me.

Cheer'd wi' the honest ploughman's sang that makes his wark nae toil—
The flocks o' sea-gulls round him as his coulter tears the soil,
When the craw-schule meets in council grave upon the furrowed lea,
Then the troutin' stream, the fishin' gad, the bonnie Tweed for me.

The modest wagtail joukin' past, wi' soft and buoyant flight,
And gurglin' streams are glancin' by, pure as the crystal bright,
When fish rise thick and three-fauld at the drake or woodcock flee,
Then the troutin' stream, the fishin' gad, the bonnie Tweed for me.

I like the merry spring, wi the bluid in nature's veins,
The dancin' streamlet's music, as it trinkles through the stanes,
The silver white upon the hook, my light gad bending free,
Wha wadna visit bonnie Tweed and share sic sport wi' me?

While there! time wings wi' speed o' thought, the day flees past sae sune,
That wha would dream o' weariness till a' the sport is dune?
We hanker till the latest blink is shed frae gloamin's e'e,
Laith, laith to quit the troutin' stream, the fishin' gad, and flee!

AWAY TO THE TWEED.

Oh! away to the Tweed,
  To the beautiful Tweed,
My much-loved native stream,
  Where the fish from his hold,
  'Neath some cataract bold,
Starts up like a quivering gleam.

To the Tweed, then, so pure,
  Where the wavelets can lure
The King of the waters to roam,
  As he shoots far and free
  Through the boundless sea,
To the halls of his silvery home.

From his iron-bound keep,
  Far down in the deep,
He holds on his sovereign sway—
  Or darts like a lance,
  Or the meteor's glance,
Afar on his bright-wing'd prey.

As he roves through the tide,
  Then his clear, glitt'ring side
Is burnish'd with silver and gold;
  And the sweep of his flight
  Seems a rainbow of light,
As again he sinks down in his hold.

Oh! then hasten with speed
  To the clear running Tweed,
The river of beauty and song,
  Where the rod swinging high
  Throws a Coldstream dress'd fly
O'er the hold of the salmon so strong.

ALEXANDER HUME.
1809-1851.

ALEXANDER HUME was a native of Kelso, where his father, Walter Hume, carried on a retail business. Little is known of his early history. The family removed from Kelso to London, and the rest of Hume's life was spent in England. His youth was a somewhat chequered period. For some months he formed one of a company of strolling players; and, being singularly gifted as a singer and an actor, he contributed very materially to the pecuniary profit of his comrades. But this kind of career did not satisfy him; and, running away under cover of night, he tramped back to London, where he succeeded in finding a more congenial sphere. About the year 1832 he connected himself with an association of young men bent on intellectual improvement, and from this time may be dated his first serious attempt at song-writing, of which a kindly critic maintained it was "musical as is Apollo's lute." For the next fifteen years or so he was absorbed in commercial undertakings, in which he was highly successful, and composed sparingly, but what he did write is sufficient to entitle him to an honourable place among the minor bards of his country. He died at Northampton in 1851. A complete edition of his *Poems and Songs* was published at London in 1845. One of Hume's best known compositions is "The Hills o' Caledonia," a lyric full of poetic power and pathos. He is not to be confounded with Alexander Hume, the author of "My ain dear Nell," and composer of the tune "Afton Water."

See Dr Roger's *Modern Scottish Minstrel* for fuller biographical notice.

THE TWEED.

O, bonnie Tweed, rin on; and may ye ever rin as clear
As ye do now in loveliness, for mony a coming year;
May ilka bonnie flower that blows, may ilka bloomless weed
That looks on ye, plead to the sun for blessings on ye—Tweed.

The gowan nestles on your banks—there hangs the stately tree,
The sheep and kye oft wander there—there sips the honey bee;
The bonnie lassies bleach their claes beside ye on the mead,
And as your waters fa' in showers, sing blessings on ye—Tweed.

The patient fisher watches ye wi' weather-beaten frame,
And muckle lippens he to you for his sweet, smiling hame;
How many happy hearts ye make, how many mou's ye feed,
The very weanies lisping pray for blessings on ye—Tweed.

There mony bonnie rivers rin in mony bonnie lands,
And mony ha'e I gazed upon, while flowing through their strands,
But O! there's ane abune them a' in beauty takes the lead,
It is yoursel', my mother stream; O! blessings on ye—Tweed.

On your sweet banks first saw I licht, I grew beside ye, stream;
Then thocht was feeling, life was like a joyous simmer dream;
But years are gane—O, heaven! I pray, here may I lay my head—
My latest breath shall melt away in blessings on ye—Tweed.

THE BRAES O' TWEEDDALE.

Air—"GLOOMY WINTER."

My blessings on ye, bonnie braes!
Ye bring up many by-gone days,

IN PRAISE OF TWEED.

As morning brings its sunny rays,
   Ye bonnie braes o' Tweeddale O!
The heart may for a time forget
The land where it and life first met,
But mem'ry, like a sun that set,
   Has ris'n again on Tweeddale O!
An' do ye ance again appear,
Ye joyous scenes o' youthfu' year—
I canna help this glad, glad tear,
   Ye bonnie braes o' Tweeddale O!

An' do we sae in gladness meet,
Ye flowers that blossom at my feet;
The very gowan seems to greet
   Wi' joy, ye braes o' Tweeddale O!
Again I bless ye, gentle things,
O' joy ye are to me the springs,
The air that sweeps o'er my heart-strings,
   Ye bonnie braes o' Tweeddale O!
I see my faither's hoose an' ha'
The wee bit bairnies in a raw,
My mother smiling through them a',
   Ye bonnie braes o' Tweeddale O!

In mony bonnie lands I 've been,
I 've gazed on mony a bonnie scene,
But O, 'mang a' that met my een,
   I met nae braes o' Tweeddale O!
The soul that dwells in mortal frame
Ne'er yearned to heaven a holier flame
Than I to you my only hame,
   Ye bonnie braes o' Tweeddale O!
As mother cleaves to her first-born,
Sae next my heart shall ye be worn;
If I forget ye, may I mourn
   A' life, ye braes o' Tweeddale O!

THOMAS TOD STODDART.

1810–1880.

THOMAS TOD STODDART, the angler-bard of the Borders, sometimes designated the "Scottish Walton," was born at Edinburgh. His father, connected by many ancestral associations with the Vale of Tweed, was a distinguished Rear-Admiral of the British Navy, who had taken part in no fewer than thirteen engagements. Entering on a course of instruction in the University, young Stoddart formed the intimate friendship of Professor Wilson, in whose class he gained the prize for a poem on "Idolatry." He became also acquainted with several eminent men of letters in the Scottish capital, who visited Wilson's house, where he was a frequent guest. In 1833 he qualified himself for the Scottish Bar, but a legal career does not seem to have had much attraction for him, as he soon abandoned it. In 1836 he contracted a somewhat romantic marriage, and settled with his wife at Kelso, a town which had a natural fascination for him from many points of view. The remainder of his life was passed here, and he died in 1880. During the forty-four years of his Kelso life he was mainly devoted to literary pursuits, and to the plying of the "gentle art." His works on angling are well-known authorities and outstanding guides on the subject. Several of his angling songs are characterised as the best of their kind ever penned.

See the delightful Memoir by his daughter, Miss Anna M. Stoddart, prefixed to *Angling Songs*. William Blackwood & Sons. 1889.

TWEED FOR EVER.

 Let ither anglers choose their ain,
  An' ither waters tak' the lead;
 O' Hielan' streams we covet nane,
  But gi'e to us the bonnie Tweed!
 An' gi'e to us the cheerfu' burn
  That steals into its valley fair—
 The streamlets that at ilka turn
  Sae saftly meet an' mingle there.

 The lanesome Talla and the Lyne,
  An' Manor wi' its mountain rills,
 An' Etterick, whose waters twine
  Wi' Yarrow frae the Forest hills;
 An' Gala, too, and Teviot bright,
  An' mony a stream o' playfu' speed;
 Their kindred valleys a' unite
  Amang the braes o' bonnie Tweed.

 There's no a hole aboon the Crook,
  Nor stane nor gentle swirl aneath,
 Nor drumlie rill nor faery brook
  That daunders through the flow'ry heath,
 But ye may find a subtle troot,
  A' gleamin' ower wi' starn an' bead,
 An' mony a sawmon sooms aboot
  Below the beilds o' bonnie Tweed.

Frae Holylee to Clovenford,
  A chancier bit ye canna hae;
Sae gin ye tak' an angler's word
  Ye'd through the whuns an' ower the brae,
An' work awa' wi' cunnin' hand
  Yer birzy hackles, black and reid;
The saft sough o' a slender wand
  Is meetest music for the Tweed!

> Oh, the Tweed! the bonnie Tweed!
>   O' rivers it's the best;
> Angle here, or angle there,
> Troots are soomin' ilka where
>   Angle east or west.

AN ANGLER'S RAMBLES.

I've angled far and angled wide,
On Fannich drear, by Luichart's side,
  Across dark Conan's current;
Have haunted Beauly's silver stream,
Where glimmering through the forest Dream
  Hangs its eternal torrent;

Among the rocks of wild Maree,
O'er whose blue billow ever free
  The daring eagles hover,
And where, at Glomach's ruffian steep,
The dark stream holds its angered leap,
  Many a fathom over;

By Lochy sad, and Laggan lake,
Where Spey uncoils his glittering snake
  Among the hills of thunder;
And I have swept my fatal fly
Where swarthy Findhorn hurries by
  The olden forest under;

IN PRAISE OF TWEED.

On Tummel's solitary bed,
And where wild Tilt and Garry wed
   In Athol's heathery valleys,
On Earn by green Duneira's bower,
Below Breadalbane's Tay-washed tower,
   And Scone's once regal palace.

There have I swept the slender line,
And where the broad Awe braves the brine,
   Have watched the grey grilse gambol,
By nameless stream and tarn remote,
With light flies in the breeze afloat,
   Holding my careless ramble.

    *   *   *   *

But dearer than all these to me
Is sylvan Tweed ; each tower and tree
   That in its vale rejoices ;
Dearer the streamlets one and all
That blend with its Eolian brawl
   Their own enamouring voices !

TWEED AND ITS PROSPECTS.

   River of all rivers, dearest
      To the Scottish heart—to ours !
   River without shade of rival,
      Rolling crystals, nursing flowers,

   Stirring up the soul of music,
      Chanting, warbling, luting, chiming,
   To the poet's ardent fancy,
      Adept in the art of rhyming;

   Marching onward through thy valley
      With the bearing of a king,
   From the hundred hills surrounding
      All thy vassals summoning !

T. T. STODDART.

DR JOHN BROWN.

GEORGE PAULIN.

JOHN RUSKIN.

IN PRAISE OF TWEED.

Of our Rivers still the Glory!
　God defend it! there is need,
For the Demon of Pollution
　Campeth on the banks of Tweed.

See the tents of the Invader!
　How they spread on every hand,
Pitched by devilish intuition
　O'er the marrow of the land!

In the fairest of its meadows,
　In its gardens of desire—
On its Bo-peeps and Blinkbonnies—
　On its terraces of Fire,

Where were fought the Fights of Freedom,
　And the stirring Songs were sung,
Which the heart and arm of Scotland
　Moved as with a trumpet tongue.

Count the forces of the Upstart,
　Smoke-begrimmed and dimly seen,
On and under the horizon,
　Blackening the blue and green.

Idle task! they multiply
　Faster than the pen can score,
Legion crowding upon legion
　Like the waves that scourge the shore.

Read the motto on their Banner:
　Self and Pelf! so apt the scroll;
Not an apter on the Headstone,
　Nor on knightly bannerol.

F

Pelf and Self! the double Demon!
  From its clutch, good God, deliver!
Save from taint of the defiler,
  Saviour! save our dearest River!

For the Life-blood of our Valleys
  We entreat on bended knee!
For the Queen of Nursing Mothers,
  God! defend her chastity!

From *Songs of the Seasons*.

TO THE TWEED.

Twined with my boyhood, wreathed on the dream
Of early endearments, beautiful stream!
The lisp of thy waters is music to me,
  Hours buried, are buried in thee.

Sleepless and sinless, the mirth of thy springs!
The light and the limpid—the fanciful things
That mingle with thine the gleam of their play,
  And are lifted in quiet away!

River! that toyest under the trees,
And lurest the leaf from the wandering breeze,
It glides over thee, like the gift of the young,
  When he rocked at the bough where it hung.

The voice of the city, the whisper of men—
I hear them, and hate them, and weary again
For the lull of the streams—the breath of the brae,
  Brought down in a morning of May.

Go! hushed o'er thy channels, the shadow'd, the dim;
Give wail for the Stricken, and worship to him
That woke the old feats of the outlaw'd and free—
  The legends that skirted on thee.

IN PRAISE OF TWEED.

Broken the shell; but its lingering tone
Lives for the stream of his fathers—his own;
And the pale wizard hand that hath gleaned out of eld,
    Is again on thy bosom beheld.

He hears not, but pilgrims that muse at his urn,
At the wailing of waters all tearfully turn
And mingle their mourning, their worship in thine,
    And gather the dews from his shrine.

Tweed! winding and wild! where the heart is unbound,
They know not, they dream not, who linger around,
How the sadden'd will smile, and the wasted re-win
    From thee—the bliss withered within.

And I, when to breathe is a burden, and joy
Forgets me, and life is no longer the boy,
On the labouring staff, and the tremorous knee,
    Will wander, bright river, to thee!

Thoughts will come back that were with me before!
Loves of my childhood left in the core,
That were hushed, but not buried—the treasured—the true,
    In memory waken anew.

And the hymn of the furze, when the dew-pearls are shed,
And the old sacred tones of thy musical bed,
Will close, as the last mortal moments depart,
    The golden gates of the heart!

From *Angling Songs*.

DR JOHN BROWN.

1810-1882.

Few names are better remembered in Scotland, or held more in honour, than good, genial, tender-hearted DR "RAB" BROWN. Great-grandson of the famous author of the *Self-Interpreting Bible*, and son of an Edinburgh divine, equally distinguished, Dr Brown was born at Biggar, in the Upper Ward of Lanarkshire. Becoming apprenticed in 1827 to Syme, the eminent surgeon, and applying himself with vigour to the study of medicine and surgery, he graduated M.D., in 1833, and at once settled down to professional life in Edinburgh. His practice never was large, 'for he was something besides a doctor, and nothing at all of a money-getter.' He died in 1882. Dr John Brown is the Charles Lamb of Scottish literature. His writings, comprised in three volumes, are among the most charming in the language. Who could be more pawky and mirth-provoking in his humour, or truer to nature in the deep touches of his pathos? He shed a halo around everything of which he wrote, and glorified, as few have been able to do, the commonest things of life. *Something about a Well* should be read in full in *Horæ Subsecivæ* (Vol. 3). The thoughtful doctor, so well deserving the title of 'the beloved physician,' preaches there one of the most eloquent and 'telling' of lay sermons.

The " Well " is that at the source of Tweed, where in the days of his Biggar callanthood the embryo essayist must often have roved.

See articles by Dr Walter Smith and Andrew Lang in *Good Words*, July, 1882, and *Century*, December, 1882 ; and *Recollections of Dr John Brown*, by Alex. Peddie, M.D., 1893.

SOMETHING ABOUT A WELL.

When a boy I knew, and often still think, of a well far up among the wild hills—alone, without shelter of wall or tree, open to the sun and all the winds. There it lies, ever the same, self-contained, all-sufficient; needing no outward help from stream or shower, but fed from its own unseen unfailing spring.

In summer, when all things are faint with the fierce heat, you may see it, lying in the dim waste, a daylight star, in the blaze of the sun, keeping fresh its circle of young grass and flowers.

The small birds know it well, and journey from far and near to dip in it their slender bills and pipe each his glad song.

The sheep-dog may be seen halting, in his haste to the uplands, to cool there his curling tongue.

In winter, of all waters, it alone lives; the keen ice that seals up and silences the brooks and shallows has no power there. Still it cherishes the same grass and flowers with its secret heat, keeping them in perpetual beauty by its soft warm breath.

Nothing can be imagined more sweetly sudden and beautiful than our well seen from a distance, set with its crown of green, in the bosom of the universal snow. One might fancy that the Infant Spring lay nestled there out of grim winter's way, waiting till he would be passed and gone.

Many a time, as a boy, have I stood by the side of this lonely well, 'held by its glittering eye,' and gazing into its black crystal depths, until I felt something like solemn fear, and thought it might be *as deep as the sea!* It was said nobody knew how deep it was, and that you might put your fishing-rod over head and not find the bottom.

But I found out the mystery. One supremely scorching summer day, when the sun was at his highest noon, I lay poring over this wonder, when behold, by the clear strong light, I saw far down, on a gentle swelling like a hill of pure white sand (it was sand), a delicate column, rising and falling and shifting in graceful measures, as if governed by a music of its own. With what awful glee did I find myself the sole witness of this spectacle! If I had caught a *Soul*, or seen *it* winking at me out of its window, I could have scarcely been more amazed and delighted.

From *Horæ Subsecivæ* (Third Series).

GEORGE PAULIN.

1812-1898.

GEORGE PAULIN was born at Horndean, in the Berwickshire parish of Ladykirk, 16th August, 1812. His forbears were Huguenots who came from France at the time of the revocation of the Edict of Nantes. He was educated at the parish school and at Selkirk, till he entered the University of Edinburgh in 1832. He was a distinguished student, and won through his diligence and outstanding literary skill the friendship of Professor Wilson (Christopher North). He became successively parish "dominie" of Newlands in Peeblesshire, and Kirknewton in Mid-Lothian. In 1844 he was appointed Rector of Irvine Academy, Ayrshire, a position which he filled with the highest acceptance until his retirement in August, 1877. In 1876 Mr. Paulin published his only volume of verse—" Hallowed Ground, and other Poems." The piece which gives title to the volume, gained the poetry prize in Wilson's class. Though resident for so many years on the western coast, it is clear that Mr Paulin never forgot the early days of his native east. He reveals now and again a cherished love for the scenes of his boyhood. Tweed still rippled in his ear, and as we read some of his finely descriptive touches, our eyes unconsciously turn to the ivy-mantled wall of Ladykirk Church, and the long row of tombstones in the churchyard beside it that bear the name of Paulin ; we catch glimpses of Horndean village, and the wooded braes and grassy haughs of Tweedside, all of which tell us that Mr Paulin, notwithstanding his long residence in Ayrshire, was still a Borderer—a Tweedsider—in spirit and affection. He died January 11th, 1898.

THE TWEED RE-VISITED.

Oh, welcome, welcome, once again, my own, my native river!
The same calm, bright blue wanderer, unchangeable as ever,
As when of yore on thy sweet banks, I thought the mighty sea
For wondrous width and soundless depth could hardly rival thee!

Thou singest still as when I heard, with hopes and feelings young,
First on thy bonnie primrose braes the water anthem sung,
And dreamed—a fond believing boy—it told of other years
When maidens gazed from castle keep on glittering Border spears.

For with my infant lullaby was blent the mighty charm
Of song that told of Flodden Field and Randolph's potent arm ;
Of English blood, from Douglas' brand washed in thy azure tide ;
And all that Border minstrelsy has warbled on Tweedside.

The same wild song thou'rt singing now, the same wild witch-notes, burst
From Memory's fount of melody, pure as they gushed at first,
When, innocent as thou, with brain unscorched by passion's fire,
To bound above thy sunlit waves was all my heart's desire.

IN PRAISE OF TWEED.

I love thee, Tweed, with deepest love—though with no headlong shock
Thou fling'st thy flashing might of waves from foamy rock to rock,
Though thou hast not sweet Teviot's charm of haugh and heathery fell,
Nor Tay's far Highland solitudes, nor Clutha's water-hell.

I love thee, for thou wanderest through a land of song and beauty
Where Loveliness is wooed by Truth, and Valour dwells with Duty—
A land of gray old castle walls and legendary lore—
A land of happy hearths and homes, where lances gleamed of yore.

I love thee, Tweed, for dear thou wert to Border Minstrels' eyes,
That often gazed with dreamy joy on thy sweet mirrored skies;
Now dim the eye and cold the brow that wore the laurel meed,
And mighty Scott and Wilson sleep as erst they sung on Tweed.

I love thee, for thou art the same thou wert in days gone by—
The cloudlets of long years ago seem floating in thy sky!
And ne'er, my native stream, may change on thy loved borders be,
Till death shall darken from my eyes this beauteous world and thee!

From *Hallowed Ground*.

THE TWEED AT ABBOTSFORD.

Pause on the bank of that melodious stream
Sacred to song. Its calm blue depths o'erhung
By woods where oft his lyre the minstrel strung,
Woo the pale moonlight's holiest, tenderest beam,

IN PRAISE OF TWEED.

Trees myriad-hued are glassed within its blue,
Embosoming a pile—a poet's thought—
A dream of old romance,—whence witchery flew
With spells for generations richly fraught,
Wrapping a world in wonder, breathing gales
From Scottish mountains on the spicy shore
Of the Carnatic, and the frozen vales
Where Highland bosoms beat in Labrador.
Within that pile *he* dwelt whose ardent soul,
Filled with bright dreams, and aspirations high,
And boundless knowledge, wonder-chained the whole
Of human kind, but turned its glorious eye
Of love on Caledon's bleak hills and cloudy sky.
——They led him forth, when sickness o'er him threw
Its soul-subduing shade, to breathe the gale
Of softer summer clime whose flowers exhale
The breath of heaven beneath its endless blue.
The hoary Alp sublime before him towered,
The Rhine to dreams of eld allured his mind.
Praise from the lips of fame was blandly poured;
They said *his* home was to no clime confined.
But, to his weary soul—'t was far away—
The heather bloomed not there by strath and stream,
He longed to feel the Tweedside breezes play,
To watch on Eildon's height the setting beam.
"Home, home," he breathed, "I must not linger here;
These scenes with exiled heart but ill accord.
O, bear me back to all to memory dear,
'T will to my faded brow be health restored,
To feel the breeze that waves the woods of Abbotsford."

From "Moral Scenery of Scotland" in *Hallowed Ground*.

JOHN RUSKIN, LL.D., D.C.L.

Born 1819.

John Ruskin, LL.D., D.C.L., the great modern apostle of art and beauty, was born in London, the only child of parents hailing originally from Scotland. Educated at Oxford, he held from 1869 to 1879, and again from 1882 to 1884, the Slade Professorship of Fine Art in that University, and has in many ways by donations of money and art treasures, as well as by his writings, exerted a great influence for true and earnest work, especially among the later generation of artists. He has been a voluminous author, and his literary style is characterised by polished and poetical gracefulness only possible in one whose mind is so wedded to the ruling passion of his life.

In the autumn of 1883 Ruskin visited Tweedside, and has set down in *Fors Clavigera*, Vol. iv., Letter xcii., his impressions of the district. [Vols. i.-viii., with full index, 1887.]

See his *Præterita*, 1885-89, one of the most charming autobiographies in the language.

THE TWEED.

I can never hear the whispering and sighing of the Tweed among his pebbles, but it brings back to me the song of my nurse, as we used to cross by Coldstream Bridge, from the south, in our happy days.

" For Scotland, my darling, lies full in my view,
With her barefooted lassies, and mountains so blue."

. . . .

As I drove from Abbotsford to Ashestiel, Tweed and Ettrick were both in flood; not dun nor wrathful, but in the clear fulness of their perfect strength; and from the bridge of Ettrick I saw the two streams join, and the Tweed for miles down the vale, and the Ettrick for miles up among his hills,—each of them, in the multitude of their windless waves, a march of infinite light, dazzling,— interminable,—intervaled indeed with eddies of shadow, but, for the most part, gliding paths of sunshine, far-swept beside the green glow of their level inches, the blessing of them, and the guard;—the stately moving of the many waters, more peaceful than their calm, only mighty, their rippled spaces fixed like orient clouds, their pools of pausing current binding the silver edges with a gloom of amber and gold; and all along their shore, beyond the sward, and the murmurous shingle, processions of dark forest, in strange majesty of sweet order, and unwounded grace of glorious age.

From *Fors Clavigera*, Letter xcii.

For a beautiful description of Ashestiel, and estimate of Sir Walter Scott's work there, see this letter in *Fors*.

The Border district of Scotland was, of all districts of the inhabited world, pre-eminently the singing country,—that which most naturally expressed its noble thoughts and passions in song.

The easily traceable reasons for this character are, I think, the following: (many exist, of course, untraceably):—

First, distinctly pastoral life, giving the kind of leisure which, in all ages and countries, solaces itself with simple music, if other circumstances are favourable,—that is to say, if the summer air is mild enough to allow repose, and the race has imagination enough to give motive to verse.

Secondly, the soldier's life, passing gradually, not in cowardice or under foreign conquest, but by his own increasing kindness and sense, into that of the shepherd; thus, without humiliation, leaving the war-wounded past to be recalled for its sorrow and its fame.

Thirdly, the extreme sadness of that past itself; giving pathos and awe to all the imagery and power of Nature.

Fourthly (this is a merely physical cause, yet a very notable one), the beauty of the sound of Scottish streams.

I know no other waters to be compared with them; such streams can only exist under very subtle concurrence of rock and climate. There must be much soft rain, not (habitually) tearing the hills down with floods; and the rocks must break irregularly and jaggedly; the pure crystal of the Scottish pebbles, giving the stream its gradations of amber to the edge, and the sound as of "ravishing division to the lute," make the Scottish fords the happiest pieces of all one's day walk. The Tweed is a beautiful river, flowing broad and bright over a bed of milk-white pebbles, unless where, here and there, it darkened into a deep pool overhung by the birches and alders which had survived the statelier growth of the primitive forest. With the murmur, whisper, and low fall of the stream, unmatched for mystery and sweetness, we must remember also the variable, but seldom wild, thrilling of the wind among the recesses of the glens; and not least, the need of relief from the monotony of occupations involving some rhythmic measure of the beat of foot or hand during the long evenings at the hearth-side.

From *Fors Clavigera*, Letter xxxii.

WILLIAM FORSYTH.
1823-1889.

WILLIAM FORSYTH was born at Earlston in 1823, and died in 1889 at Bridge-of-Allan, whither he had gone for the benefit of his health. His life was passed in the towns of Galashiels, Edinburgh, Aberdeen, and Glasgow, in which latter city he originated and managed for twenty-five years the well-known Cobden Hotel. In 1885 he stood as Liberal candidate for the Bridgeton division of Glasgow, but was defeated. He was a keen angler, and published in 1887 *A Lay of Loch Leven*, dedicated to the Glasgow Anglers' Association. He wrote many lyrical pieces of much sweetness and power, and was the intimate acquaintance of several eminent literary men.

See *Minstrelsy of the Merse*, pp. 183-186.

THE TWEED.

Come, gentle Tweed ! accept my lay,
  Which on thy banks I framed reclining:
Long years have lapsed since first the day
  I listened to thy waters chiming:
Years which have brought enough of change,
  The lights and shades of life combining;
Long years through which old memories range,
  And fade not though my day's declining.

IN PRAISE OF TWEED.

Less change in you than change in me:
 Thy sparkle is as bright as ever;
Thy flowering meadows fringing thee,
 Embrace thee still, dear limpid river!
The sportive lambs on sunny knowes,
 Still frisk and frolic, full of gambol;
The linnet chants from 'midst thy howes,
 To cheer his mate 'mong broom or bramble.

The trout leaps in thy gleaming tide:
 The chirming ousels search thy shallows,
And o'er thy bounteous bosom wide
 Career in flocks the fleet-wing'd swallows.
Thy woody banks, where all is still,
 Except the birds that through them flutter:
The shepherd lingers on the hill
 To listen what thy streams may utter.

And what are now the strains he hears,
 Upborne through mists round mountains hoary?
No sighs nor sounds which woke the fears
 Oft murmured in thine ancient story.
Sweet peace now crowns thy past'ral plains—
 No reivers' clamour, feudal struggle;
From happy homes thy frugal swains
 Safe tend their flocks and list thy gurgle.

When first I ranged thy classic heights,
 And saw thee wind 'mid woodlands gleaming,
That feeling still my soul delights,
 Like one who clings to pleasant dreaming.
From Neidpath Fell I first looked o'er
 Quaint Ashestiel, the theme of story,
Where Scott did over "Marmion" pore,
 His hero sent in quest of glory.

WILLIAM FORSYTH.

WALTER C. SMITH.

C. M. DAWSON.

PROFESSOR VEITCH.

IN PRAISE OF TWEED.

From Laidlawstiel's brown sun-burnt hills,
   For Holylee a rampart fitting,
That softly nestles 'tween the rills,
   Which leapt from craigs where I was sitting,
To swell thy tide that fondly laves
   Round Elibank of matchless beauty;
Where coy you check your rippling waves,
   Pay tribute as a loving duty.

Sweetly embosomed 'mong soft trees,
   No wonder though you long to tarry,
And loving turn, oft ill at ease,
   Its farewell greeting forth to carry.
Its bloom and beauty all are yours,
   As long as time and tide keep rolling,
With daily access to its bowers,
   While down thy song-crowned valleys strolling.

But I, alas! how reft and lone:
   My heart with all its bright hopes baffled,
My nearest and my dearest gone;
   Each tie of friendship snapt or ruffled,
I turn to thee, my much-loved stream;
   I find no traces of thy sorrow;
As amorous of the sun's bright beam
   As thou wert on thy natal morrow.

I turn to thee; thy presence oft
   Has sooth'd me when with anguish riv'n;
Thy pensive calm bore me aloft,
   With impulse still as if from heaven.
Roll on, fair stream! I soon must leave—
   Roll through each mead and cherished valley
To part from thee I may not grieve,
   For thou from year to year wilt rally.

IN PRAISE OF TWEED.

The day will come I'll know no spring,
  Nor see thee in thy summer grandeur,
Which to thy banks each year will bring:
  With shortening step, I westward wander,
But thy majestic, ceaseless swell
  Will gather friendships round thee ever,
When short-lived inmates of each dell
  Will cease to know thee, noble river!

From *The Border Counties' Magazine.*—Galashiels, November, 1881.

WALTER CHALMERS SMITH, D.D., LL.D.

Born 1824.

WALTER CHALMERS SMITH, D.D., LL.D., was born at Aberdeen in 1824, studied at Old Aberdeen and Edinburgh, and, after holding the Presbyterian charge of Islington in London for some years, laboured as a minister of the Free Church at Orwell in Kinross-shire, in Edinburgh, in Glasgow, and again in Edinburgh in the Free High Church, from the pastorate of which he retired in 1897. In 1867 he was tried for heresy, but the charge was dismissed. He was Moderator of the Free Church General Assembly in 1893. He is widely known and esteemed as a preacher and as an accomplished man of letters. His poetry, of which he has published close on a dozen volumes, is characterised by great richness of thought, creative imagination, and lyrical charm.

See *The Bishop's Walk and the Bishop's Times*, by "Orwell," 1861; *Olrig Grange*, 1872; *Borland Hall*, 1874; *Hilda : among the Broken Gods*, 1878; *Raban, or Life-Splinters*, 1881; *North Country Folk*, 1883; *Kildrostan*, 1884; *A Heretic and other Poems*, 1891; and his *Selected Poems*, 1893.

DRYBURGH.

Meet resting-place by his belovéd Tweed,
Amid the graceful ruins of old time,
For him whose wizard spell of potent rhyme
Brought back the old time, with its heroic deed
And charm of beauty. Slender as a reed
Is the slim pillar on the transept tall,
Where the lush wall-flower blooms, and over all
A rowan grows, where some wind-wafted seed
Had lodged, and all is silent as a dream,
But for a throstle on the ancient yew,
But for the low faint murmur of the stream ;
And sweet old-fashioned scents are floating through
The arch from thyme and briar, as for ever
Shall his sweet nature haunt this fabled river.

From *The River Tweed from its Source to the Sea*, by Sir George Reid, *P*.R.S.A., and Professor Veitch, 1884.

CHRISTOPHER MURRAY DAWSON.
BORN 1826.

CHRISTOPHER MURRAY DAWSON, F.E.I.S., F.G.S., is a native of Cupar-Fife, and at the age of four years came with his parents to reside at Coldstream, in which ancient Border town his boyhood and youth were passed. He was trained as a pupil teacher, and in 1844 became assistant English Master in Madras Academy at Cupar. Two years later he was appointed master of Abercorn School, a picturesque village by the Firth of Forth. Here he lived for forty-three years, retiring in 1889, and taking up his abode in Edinburgh. He published in 1891 "Avonmore and other Poems," the fruit of leisure moments throughout many years. Mr Dawson is devoted to all that pertains to the Border Country. The Tweed at Coldstream, and the old town are full of tender memories, and through the mists of more than sixty years he can look back on many a sweet vision of that happy past.

See *Minstrelsy of the Merse*, pp. 239-245, and *Poets of Linlithgowshire*, pp. 133-144.

THE TWEED AT COLDSTREAM.

I cannot turn, O Tweed, from thee,
  I lingering look behind;
Yet all have sunk into the past
  That link thee to my mind;
For what hath time now left to me
But memories of love and thee?

IN PRAISE OF TWEED.

Thy waters roll as proudly now
    As when I was a boy,
And still unchanged thy sunlit scenes
    That gave my life its joy;
I see along thy winding shore
The dear old spots just as of yore.

But where are they who played with me,
    Who made this holy ground,
Whose names are whispered by the breeze
    And echoed all around?
I hear their voices rise to-day
Like angel music far away.

And they who taught my troubled soul,
    'Mid doubt's o'erwhelming strife,
To feel not time, nor yet the grave,
    The Omega of life?
O, from yon cloud-land let them rise,
And bless me 'mid my tear-dimmed eyes.

Thy silver willows swinging still,
    In cadence to thy song,
Press amorous kisses on thy waves,
    As swift they glide along;
While down beneath their shadows rest
    A softer forest in thy breast.

How strange, O Tweed, thy magic power
    Fills all around with friends,
And ties long snapped by widening years
    Rejoin their broken ends;
The past returns, and on thy shore
My childhood days I live once more.

For, looking on thy sunny waves,
   All wrapped in flickering gold,
I throw away the rust of years
   And feel not that I'm old;
And long-lost joys each spot invest,
And clothe all in a golden mist.

Hope smiled on sunny waters then,
   With rapture in her eye,
And all around, where'er I turned,
   A glorious earth and sky,
And life was wreathed in gorgeous beams,
Yet pure as holy angels' dreams.

The dews of life's young morning fell
   So soft on Hope's young root,
That none e'er dreamed such promise fair
   Would yield such bitter fruit,
Or prove our lives a chess-board game,
Victor or vanquished all the same!

O life! O vanished years and dreams!
   Where heaven, were you to last?
Your loves were blessed angel-guests,
   And these, O Tweed, are past;
And in dear memory's hallowed land
They make a silent shadow-band.

Away regret! Life has a goal,
   A purpose and a prize,—
Love welling out to guilt or woe,
   Love quickened from the skies,
Living for men, easing their load,
Leading their footsteps on to God

From *Avonmore and Other Poems.*

ON RE-VISITING TWEEDSIDE.

Thrice dear old scenes, proud Borderland!
   Home of the true and brave,
Where Freedom found a swift right hand,
   Her hallowed shrine to save;
Thy sons from stricken fields would come,
With hope unquenched for hearth and home.

What ballad lore and weirds of fate,
   And love songs fill thy vales,
While bloody trysts and clansmen's hate
   Ghost all thy lonely dales;
Even here, our pensive step may tread
Some unknown hero's silent bed.

O sunny lands of love and dreams!
   I bless thy heritage,
When youth pulsed through these aged limbs,
   And hope, with holy rage,
Sang her proud song—an angel lay,
Life's path all sunshine—toil all play!

Thy glories moulded every thought,
   Life thrilled each light and shade,
And Fancy's fingers through them sought
   For truths that cannot fade;
And in my hours of loving toil,
These were a store of endless spoil;
Free from my lips they joyous fell
On children's ears that loved them well.

I caught the wild notes of thy fells,
   The music of thy streams;
Thy storms were songs; thy winds' fierce swells
   Gave voices to my dreams;
They threw a weird-born thrall o'er me,
And in their freedom I was free.

Thy abbeys haunting all thy vales
  Rose ever one vast prayer,
Where hearts would fight through mists to God,
  And find sweet refuge there;
While every stream from moor and glen
Would softly chant its dear Amen!

Vain man would hedge his father's God,
  Bind love to narrow creed,
And spurn who tread another road,
  As worse than poison-weed;
Thy preachers with a mighty voice
In broader love made me rejoice.

God's sun shone on Tweed's sister strands,
  Old England shared his smiles,
And Scotland basked her mountain-lands,
  Her meads and dark defiles;
While birds from different shores would mate,
And on one Father's bounty wait;
Till 'shivering Lap and sunburnt Moor'
Rose brothers mine—heirs of one store.

JOHN VEITCH, LL.D.

1829-1894.

JOHN VEITCH, LL.D., one of the most prominent Border patriots of recent times, was born at Peebles on the 24th October, 1829. Educated first at an adventure school, and afterwards at the Grammar School of his native burgh, he passed, in 1845, to the University of Edinburgh, of which he became one of its most distinguished students. It was the dream of his parents that he should study for the ministry of the Free Church of Scotland, and in 1850 we find him commencing certain theological classes with the view of carrying out that intention, "but these were soon dropped, not that they lost favour with him, for he retained the keenest interest in religious questions, and would trenchantly discuss them to the end of his days. But the ecclesiastical atmosphere was uncongenial, and finally helped to determine his strong bent to philosophical liberty." In 1856 he became assistant to Sir William Hamilton, in the Edinburgh Logic chair, and after his death, in the same year, to his successor, Professor Alexander Campbell Fraser. Four years later he was appointed successor to Professor Spalding in the chair of Logic, Rhetoric, and Metaphysics, at St Andrews, and in 1864 he was translated to the chair of Logic and Rhetoric in the University of Glasgow, which he held until his death on 3rd September, 1894. By dint of plodding and of unflinching perseverance, John Veitch rose to high eminence as a professor, a philosopher, a poet, and a historian. While he made many noteworthy contributions to the philosophical literature of his day, it is not as an exponent of any system of philosophy that he will be best remembered. No one, next to Walter Scott, ever wrote or sang so sweetly of the heroic age of the Scottish Lowlands. The Tweed and its tributaries, the hills and glens, the spreading moorlands, with the memories of the past in ruined tower and castled crag, sent him singing and writing of his Border home; and through his rugged but matchless eloquence other souls were thrilled with the witching spell of the Borders. How many there are who can trace to his stirring words, both by mouth and pen, an increasing reverence for all that is good and noble and beautiful in the history and romance of the Border Country! He has given us the finest history of Border life, the truest interpretation of Scottish and Border poetry, and made doubly dear to the Border memory the weird stories and traditions, the romantic songs and ballads that gather so thickly round this glamour-haunted land.

See *Memoir of John Veitch, LL.D.*, by his Niece, Mary R. L. Bryce. Edinburgh: W. Blackwood, 1896.

Professor R. M. Wenley's INTRODUCTION to Veitch's *Dualism and Monism*. Edinburgh, 1895.

And also the following:—*Hillside Rhymes*, 1872. *The Tweed, and other Poems*, 1875. *History and Poetry of the Scottish Border*, first edition, one volume, 1878; second edition, two volumes, 1893. *The Feeling for Nature in Scottish Poetry*, two volumes, 1887. *Merlin, and other Poems*, 1889. *Border Essays*, 1896.

THE TWEED.

FROM SUMMER MORN TO EVE, MAY 9, 1886.

Come bright in the morn's beam,
   Come joyous and free,
Brave son of the moorland,
   My heart speeds with thee.

Through gleaming pool stately,
   Then rushing in stream,
Ye pass, lightly changing
   As moods in a dream.

Green alders, birk tresses,
   Fleck thy waves as they glide;
The cloud-gleams are borne on
   Thy pure lapsing tide.

Meet spirit for worship,
   Sky-born and earth-given,
Thou minglest earth's shades with
   The hues of the heaven.

Thine the joy of the morning,
   Thine gleam of bright day;
Till grey-coming gloamin'
   Greets thee on thy way,

And spreads her veil o'er thee,
   Withdrawn from our eyes,—
And we hear thy voice moving
   In soft fall and rise.

While earth's sounds are hushed all
In the mild even's calm,
And the stars and I listen
Thy heaven-borne psalm.

From *Merlin, and Other Poems.*

THE TWEED.

'Mid uplands first to wear the gleam of morn,
And spread the early sheen of dewy grass,
While sweet wild flowers are breathing odours free,
And clear, air-borne, pathetic bleatings float,
And pewit's cry is heard, half-wail, half-wile—
Voice dear unto the heart of solitude—
And heron stalks, then slow majestic sails
Away short space, on low broad flapping wing;—
A lovely Well uprises, sacred, clear,
Thine own, historic Tweed, the fount amid
The bent of thy first runlet life of sound.

A tiny rill of still uncertain fate,
To be perchance soon lost in larger stream,
Or sink unnoticed 'mid the peaty hags,
Like to a broken life that ends in gloom;
Or, fitting symbol of a perfect lot,
Grow a great river, bear a glorious name,
Reflect to many eyes of short-lived men,
Age after age as they pass o'er the earth,
The high pure lights of God, and flowing flash
Heaven-borrowed splendour throughout all the land

A streamlet, thou, in latent purpose strong,
A line of force in far south-west that springs,
Aye tending steadfast to the north-east sea,

As thereto moved by phantasy innate,
Or drawn by love of morning's early gleam,
And sun uprising o'er the dappled hills;
But here at distant source who can foresee
A purpose in thy tiny wave, far less
That thou wilt e'er rejoice o'er compassed aim?
Thou 'rt as a human life, but just awake
To feeling 'mid the world's blank, lonely wild,
That gropes all darkly for its fate, and finds
Its end in groping; effort blind becomes
Illumed in act, the life grows free and full
Through striving forces fused: and here, slight rill,
Thou seek'st a way 'mid strong contending streams,
That numerous rush from high confronting glens;
Now nobly is thine impulse full upborne
By loyal south-west flow, and then again
Bent backwards from thy course by north-east burn;
And yet from conflict thou e'er risest strong,
Nay, in thy soft green haughs mak'st gleaming peace,
For there is one fair harmony of flow,
Thou still'st the war of waters from the heights,
And in the reconcilement of the streams,
Grow'st to an ampler life, serener tide,
Till, in accomplished aim, thou glidest grand,
In triumph and in tribute to the sea!

Thy lot it is, fair Stream, to flow amid
A varied vale: not mountain height alone,
Nor mere outspreading flat is dully thine,
But wavy lines of hills, high, massive, broad,
That rise and fall, and flowing softly fuse
In haughs of grassy sward, a deep-hued green;
No call thou mak'st on dwellers by thy banks
To constant struggle with mere mountain-steeps,
Nor leav'st them all to indolence of dreams
On pastoral plain; but, mingling hill and dale

IN PRAISE OF TWEED.

And gleaming pool, like that old Attic land,
Where thought and fancy reached their perfect type,
Thou hast evoked full human energy,
Yet charmed it by sweet breaks of soft repose;
By thee have many lives in quiet passed
Of staid demeanour and of manly mood,
Content with circle of mere homely deeds,
And yet inspiréd deep by breath of song,
That carols now with lark at flush of morn,
Then moves soft-toned, subdued, as hallowed eve
Glows in the west, and dies beyond the hills.

Down many a sky-arched, hill-enfolded glen,
Where summer shadows dwell with mountain sounds,
The speeding stream, uncharmed to rest by birk
That woos it, fair forget-me-not's sweet eyes,
The moss sun-hued, with sparkle as of tears,
The glow of heathery brae, the bracken sheen,
And unarrested by the deep grey rock
That only stirs it to a quicker flow—
Makes haste to greet thee, Tweed, in verdant haugh,
And with its tribute swells thine early wave.

By heritage, pure Tweed, of haugh and hill,
Which thou possessest with a lordly mien,
From thy high Well to where the ocean tide
Speeds through the arches that two kingdoms bridge,
To greet thine upland wave—by sunny gleams
Along thy gliding path, by sweep of stream,
And alder-shaded pools,—long hast thou wooed
Thy sons to heart-felt love of earth and heaven;
Silent their love has often been, but deep,
As finding no meet voice, known but to thee,
O noble stream, and those whose hearts were thine!
Chief thou dost teach, by solitude of glens,
And wonders of the sky, the shepherd lad

IN PRAISE OF TWEED.

Who ever haunts thy hills, till in him grows
The deep impassioned heart, and in quaint phrase
He graphic sets both what he sees and feels—
Sometimes in awe, sometimes in stirring love—
Of daily wonders all around his path,
Not for him wonders, rather daily food,
Unconscious nurture of the inner soul
That gropes amid sense-visions for its God!

How pure the guardian Genius of the Stream!
Of bright and gentle face in summer tide,
In flow robed clear as heaven's own gracious light;
And with a strength that keeps the mastery
Of self, Tweed rushes bold in joy of break,
And then glides on sedate and calm in pool;
Yet often marks the changes of our lot,
For grey-cloud shadows, sudden, throw a veil
Of wavering sadness o'er the water's face;
And, in the gloamin', long wan silent pools
Speak a mysterious sympathy with grief,
As though the stream were widowed of the sun.

And late in Autumn, when the mists have come,
And the dark clouds lie low on all the heights,
And brown decay has seized the wasting leaves,
In troubled flow, O Tweed, thou risest strong,
As 'neath the mighty burden of the skies,
At call of waters hoarse and sounding burns;
Then unrestrained and unimpeded sweep'st,—
By the stern spirit of the hills deep moved,—
To stir the grander pulses of our heart,
And thrill us with the rushing sense of power,
And firmly nerve our souls for high exploits.

On Winter's night, when eye can nought discern
Of shape of things, and ear is all alert,

ALEXANDER SMITH.

JOHN TODD.

J. B. SELKIRK.

JOHN DICKSON.

IN PRAISE OF TWEED.

I 've heard thee hurrying shout in swoop of flood,—
With voice that rose and fell, and quelled the vale,
As if there surged a people's battle-din.

Tweed! most thy gentle spirit loves the smile
Of heaven's own face,—amid the dappled light
Of Spring, when soft white showers, from passing clouds
That mottle light the blue of space o'erhead,
First glisten on the green of birken leaves,
And sprinkle all the haughs with twinkling rain;
While, in the sunny blinks between the showers,
The primrose blessing sends from woody braes,
The linnet strains its note to voice the joy
That pulses in the air; the sounding stream
For very gladness gleams; the speckled trout,
Drawn from dark depths of winter pools, disport
In overflow of life and innocence,
And, 'neath the airy insects' sun-bright dance,
Make quiet circlings o'er the spreading face,
Complacent, of the pool with pleasure moved.

For many a day, the Spirit of the Stream
Thus softly spake to eye and heart of man,
Unvoiced, unsung; circled, in breathing Spring,
Around grim towers, where life was watchful, hard,
And heedless of the joy the birds proclaimed.
In Summer, spread green haughs and meadows soft
For gentle lowing kine; and flushed the vale
With bloom, the symbol of the year's full strength,
The flower of perfect life; and sought to move
To tender thought, by Autumn's mellow look
On waning birks, that, 'mid the dwining light
Of late October, gently lay aside
Their bravery green, and beautifully die.

How clear thy ripple, Tweed! this dewy morn,
As clear as if thou now rejoicing sprung,

H

At thy first birth, from confines of the hills,
And all the myriad years were still to come
Of storm and sunshine, troubled sounds and floods,
That yet have moved all traceless o'er thy face!
Art thou the same through those long chequer'd years?
Immortal, 'mid the mortal lives of men!
As ever-gleaming truth 'mid passing shows!
Or dost thou die each eve amid the gloom,
When slow I see thee fade and pass away,
Thou and the Sun—and both are born afresh
With each new morn, new-births, God-purified?
To me, nor Sun nor Stream has tinge of eld.
Thou, River, but the white and aimless mists
Upon the hills, each morn by God's own hand
Up-gathered calm to one pure flowing life;
Thou, Sun! each morn new made, the orbéd sum
Of the vague glow and scattered fires of dawn,—
River and Sun, the symbols of a Hand
That opes and shuts each day upon the world,—
Both old as Death, and yet as young as Youth!

From *The Tweed and Other Poems.*

ALEXANDER SMITH.

1830-1867.

ALEXANDER SMITH, a brilliant literary genius whose sun all too quickly set, was born at Kilmarnock, on 31st December, 1830. His father was a designer of patterns for lace, and the son, though wishful to study for the ministry, was obliged through ill-health to abandon that hope and to follow the same profession. He began life in a Glasgow warehouse, and filled up his leisure hours with a large amount of literary work. Poems from his pen appeared in many of the local newspapers, such as the *Glasgow Citizen*, etc. In 1852 he created quite a sensation in literary circles by the publication of his *Life Drama*, which had been well "boomed" by no less a critic than George Gilfillan. Smith had just turned twenty, and for a time it looked as if the new poet had come to remain. He was praised and flattered by hosts of admirers. Ten thousand copies of the work were sold in a few months. In 1854 the author was appointed Secretary to the University of Edinburgh, a dignified and lucrative post which he held until his death. But his popularity as a poet was short-lived. He awoke, like Byron, to find himself famous, but did not fulfil the rich promise that had been formed of his capabilities. The faults of the *Life Drama* began to be apparent. It was considered to be too immature and extravagant, whilst there were those who did not hesitate to bring against him the viler charge of plagiarism, so closely did his lines of thought and turns of expression follow in the wake of some of the modern writers. He met, it must be admitted, with but scant treatment at the hands of his critics; yet he was by no means devoid of merit, and was worthy of more grateful recognition. In 1857 he wrote *City Poems*, and some years afterwards a Northumbrian epic, *Edwin of Deira*, and *Alfred Hagart's Household*, a simple and pathetic tale of Scottish middle-class life. Some of his productions have been surpassed by few poets of his time, for the depth of feeling and artistic genius that pervades them. Gerald Massey went the length of styling Smith the "Rubens among poets." As an essayist Smith took at once a foremost position, and many who attacked him as a poet, welcomed his appearance in this new capacity. *Dreamthorp* and *A Summer in Skye* will long remain two of the most charming essay collections one could wish to meet with. He died at Wardie, near Edinburgh, 8th January, 1867.

See *Memoir* by Patrick Proctor Alexander, prefixed to *Last Leaves* (1869), and the Rev. T. Brisbane's *Early Years of Alexander Smith* (1869).

AT PEEBLES.

I lay in my bedroom at Peebles,
    With my window curtains drawn,
While there stole over hill of pasture and pine
    The unresplendent dawn.

And through the deep silence I listened,
    With a pleased, half-waking heed,
To the sound which ran through the ancient town—
    The shallow-brawling Tweed.

For to me 't was a realisation
    Of dream ; and I felt like one
Who sees first the Alps, or the Pyramids,
    World-old, in the setting sun ;

First, crossing the purple Campagna,
    Beholds the wonderful dome
Which a thought of Michael Angelo hung
    In the golden air of Rome.

And all through the summer morning
    I felt it a joy indeed
To whisper again and again to myself,
    This is the voice of the Tweed.

Of Dryburgh, Melrose, and Neidpath,
    Norham Castle brown and bare,
The merry sun shining on merry Carlisle,
    And the Bush aboon Traquair,

I had dream'd : but most of the river,
    That, glittering mile on mile,
Flow'd through my imagination,
    As through Egypt flows the Nile.

Was it absolute truth, or a dreaming
  That the wakeful day disowns,
That I heard something more in the stream, as it ran,
  Than water breaking on stones?

Now the hoofs of a flying mosstrooper,
  Now a bloodhound's bay, half-caught,
The sudden blast of a hunting-horn,
  The burr of Walter Scott.

Who knows? But of this I am certain,
  That but for the ballads and wails
That make passionate dead things, stocks and stones,
  Make piteous woods and dales,

The Tweed were as poor as the Amazon,
  That, for all the years it has roll'd,
Can tell but how fair was the morning red,
  How sweet the evening gold.

From *A Summer in Skye.*

JOHN TOD.

Born 1832.

John Tod, so well known by his pen-name of "John Strathesk," is a native of Lasswade, Mid-Lothian, where he still resides, of which village his paternal forbears had been residenters for more than four generations. On his mother's side his associations are chiefly with the upper Tweed valley in the parishes of Tweedsmuir, Broughton, and Drumelzier. Than Mr Tod, few men are more intimately acquainted with this portion of the Southern Highlands. He has climbed almost every hill-top, and fished in almost every stream. The Tweed and its tributaries are for him full of happy memories, and it is a singular pleasure to hear him descant on the history and romance of the district, or recount the personal incidents pertaining to a later day. Notwithstanding a somewhat busy life, Mr Tod has found opportunity for a large amount of literary work. *Bits from Blinkbonny; or, Bell o' the Manse: a tale of Scottish village life between* 1841 *and* 1851, has been most cordially received by many thousands of sympathetic readers, and has been translated into several languages. He has also written *More Bits from Blinkbonny*—Scottish village life between 1831 and 1841—*Little Bluebird, the Girl Missionary; Miss Graham's 'Protégé,' Elder Logan's Story* about the Kirks, Bits about America, Andrew Gillon: a Tale of the Covenanters, Glentirlie, The "Come" and "Go" Family Text-Book, and many racy newspaper articles.

TWEEDLE-DUM AND TWEEDLE-DEE.

Tune—"*Oh! but ye've been lang o' comin'.*"

Could man or fisher wish for more?
   The Tweed has troots and tales galore,
O' rhymes and salmon sic a store;
      The "Fisher's Tryst" o' Scotland.

Frae Ericstane's far drearie Well,
   She sings an' brattles down the dell,
An' blithely gathers to hersel'
      The bonniest burns in Scotland.

The Talla brown, the Manor clear;
   The laughing Leithen, flowery Quair;
The Ettrick wed to Yarrow rare;
      The Fairyland o' Scotland.

The Gala gay, the Leader sweet;
   The sullen Till, the siller Te'it;
The "Adders" twa baith swell and greet
      The Tweed, the gem o' Scotland.

The heather hills, the Yarrow birks;
   Traquair's "Tryst Bush," auld Forest kirks,
An' "peels," an' abbeys, grace the lirks
      O' Tweed, the Harp o' Scotland.

IN PRAISE OF TWEED.

Her martyrs, rhymers, shepherds, bards,
  Her Elibanks an' Abbotsfords,
Lang, lang will be the fireside words
    O' hut and ha' in Scotland.

Oh ye that hap mankind wi' "tweeds,"
  We like the claith, but hate your deeds:
For your black " saps," " Our mither" bleeds,
    Ye smear the pride o' Scotland.

Fishers ha'e hearts. Eh! Cowdenknowes,
  An' Smailholm Tower, and Lonely Lowes,
An' hills, an' dales, an' "hopes," an' howes
    Ye 're dear to us—to Scotland.

Flow on, old Tweed, by Cot an' Ha'
  Your "Flowers" are no' "a' wede awa',"
Come fishin' time, we 'll gi 'e a ca';
    Ye bear the gree in Scotland.

From *Glentirlie*—1890.

"J. B. SELKIRK."
BORN 1832.

JAMES BROWN, better known by his literary name of J. B. Selkirk, was born at Selkirk, where he still resides (1898). He was educated at Selkirk, and at The Edinburgh Institution. Few names are better known throughout the Border country. All his life enthusiastically devoted to Border literature, his own contributions thereto, both in prose and verse, are amongst the brightest treasures that have been added to the pile. No one, certainly, has penned so many delightful songs of Yarrow, all of them gems of the singer's art. His *Song of Yarrow* will compare any day with Wordsworth's three Yarrow ballads. He is the one native of the Forest who has been able to read "the secret" of its river of dool and sorrow, and to give to it that masterly interpretation only possible in a writer of the highest gift. So long as Yarrow brattles to the Ettrick, untouched by any other save the hand of Nature, so long as it sheds its witchery around the wanderer amongst the Forest hills, so long will " J. B. Selkirk's " name be associated with it. He has contributed extensively to magazine literature, and is the author of the following works :—

Bible Truths with Shakesperian Parallels. Longmans, 1862.
Poems. Longmans, 1869.
Ethics and Esthetics of Modern Poetry. Smith, Elder, & Co., 1878.

Yarrow and other Poems.   Kegan Paul, Trench, & Co., 1883.
Poems.   Wm. Blackwood & Sons, 1896.
See also *The Secret of Yarrow* article in *Blackwood*, 1886.

WHERE TWEED FLOWS DOWN.

Where Tweed flows down by Cadonlee,
   And slowly seeks a deepening bed,
I stand alone, a blighted tree.

From me no more, as all men see,
   Shall bud go forth, or leaf be shed,
Where Tweed flows down by Cadonlee.

Since that wild night of storm, when she
   From all her happy kindred fled,
I stand alone, a blighted tree.

Deep in the night she came to me,
   Hands clenched above her fallen head,
Where Tweed flows down by Cadonlee.

And holding still the fatal key
   Of that grim secret, dark and dread,
I stand alone, a blighted tree.

Before the black pool held its dead,
I heard the last wild word she said !—
I stand alone, a blighted tree,
Where Tweed flows down by Cadonlee.

From *Poems*, 1896 edition.

JOHN DICKSON.

Born 1833.

John Dickson was born at Lessudden, March 13, 1833. He has been resident in Glasgow for over forty years, where he carried on a successful business, from which he has recently retired. Poetry is one of his hobbies, and his Tweed verses have long been popular in Border gatherings. He is now (1898) the oldest active member of any Border Association.

BONNIE TWEED.

O' a' the braid rivers that rin to the sea,
By muirland an' mountain, through valley an' lea,
That glide through the woodland, or wind through the mead,
There's nane o' them a' like our ain bonnie Tweed.

In days o' lang syne, when to sport in her streams
Was my summer day's joy and my summer nicht's dreams,
I played wi' her waves, and o' time took nae heed;
She ne'er wearied wi' me, nor me wi' the Tweed.

And when wi' the summer-spate drumlie she ran,
And I watch'd for her clearin' till nicht-fa' began,
Then dowie an' lanely I pillow'd my head
An' dream'd I was chas'd wi' big waves o' the Tweed.

O, sweet o'er the haugh rings the milk-maiden's sang,
And the reed o' the shepherd the green knowes amang,
But to me sweeter music than sang or than reed
Is the ripple that breaks on the bosom o' Tweed.

Yet, tho' through this life's course I weel nigh ha'e sped,
And friends ha'e grown few and companions ha'e fled,
O'er her clear flowin' waters nae change seems decreed,
Eld downa lay hands on the wavelets o' Tweed.

And when o'er the stream o' this life I ha'e pass'd
And be kindly laid down for my lang sleep and last,
'Neath the auld kirkyard tree, oh, may mine be the meed,
To be crooned to my rest by the murmur o' Tweed !

From *The Border Magazine.*

"A. G."

1835.

IN *Blackwood*, vol. xxxviii., page 247. "The poem, 'To the River Tweed' is entered in the Magazine Contributors' Book as 'Anon, per Professor Wilson.'"

Note to Editor from Mr William Blackwood, January, 1898.

TO THE RIVER TWEED.

Roll on, bright Tweed! roll on,
  And let thy waters be
A tribute to the many waves
  Of the dark and heaving sea!
Many clear winding streams
  On thy broad bosom meet,
And the sea with gentle murmurings
  Their mingled tides will greet.
Roll on, then, Tweed, until they be
Lost in the waves of the deep dark sea!

Thy banks are rich and fair,
  Thy woods wave green and wild,
And thou bearest many a roving rill,
  The distant mountain's child.
Roll on, then, kingly river,
  By castle, hall, and tower—
By palace proud and lowly cot—
  By greenwood, glen, and bower
Roll on, roll on, until you gain
The wild waves of the restless main!

IN PRAISE OF TWEED.

As by thy sunlit waters
  With wondering eyes I stand,
And gaze on all the varied scenes
  Of this fair pleasant land,
I think—bright, flowing river—
  How much has come and gone
While on thy wide and winding path
  Thou hast been rolling on ;
Still rolling on, unchanged and free,
To the bounding waves of the deep dark sea.

How many eyes are closed in death,
  How many hearts are cold,
How many youthful forms have sunk
  Between the grey and old.
How many in those scattered homes
  Have come and passed away—
Fleeting and fair, as the bright sun's beams,
  Or like the meteor's ray—
Whose course through time passed on like thee
To the billows of eternity.

Peace be to thy blue waters,
  As with gentle song they flow ;
Light be the breath of the whispering winds
  When on thy shores they blow,
May the blue sun's dancing rays
  On thy rippling wavelets gleam,
And gladsome be thy pilgrimage,
  Thou, brightly flowing stream !
Roll on, in beauty, till you gain
The white waves of the restless main.

From *Blackwood's Magazine*, August, 1835.

ALEXANDER BROWN.
Born 1837.

ALEXANDER BROWN was born at Lochhead, a farm in the Fifeshire parish of Auchtertool. After receiving a fair elementary education at the village school of Lochgelly, he was sent, at the age of fourteen, to Milnathort to learn the trade of cabinet-making. He removed to Edinburgh in 1857, where he still pursues that calling. His leisure hours are filled with reading and literary work, and he has been a very frequent contributor to periodical literature. Mr Brown's verse has invariably in it an even and steady gracefulness, characterised by refined feeling, and a rich depth of thought.

See *The Scottish Poets, Recent and Living*, by A. G. Murdoch, 1883, pp. 302-309.

AN AUTUMN DAY AT NEIDPATH.

To-day I rove as fancy wills,
  By scenes of old renown ;
What time the purple on the hills,
  Is fading into brown.

When in the mellow Autumn glow,
  The land its richest yields ;
And woodlands daily darker grow,
  Around the harvest fields,

IN PRAISE OF TWEED.

The odours of the pine wood blow
   Around me where I lie,
And watch the clear and placid flow
   Of Tweed glide softly by;

Where Neidpath's hoary tower is seen,
   Bereft by time and foe;
Look proudly from its banks of green,
   Into the stream below.

What shadowy pageants of the past!
   What gleams of ancient rule!
The vanished centuries have cast
   Upon this glassy pool.

Here captives passed to dungeons dark,
   And love watched from the towers;
And warriors left their iron mark,
   In sterner times than ours.

And here when night crept up the stream,
   Red as a baleful star,
The warder caught the fiery gleam
   Of danger from afar.

But all to-day is like a dream,
   Of days when war shall cease;
And rippling in the sun's bright beam,
   The river murmurs, peace.

The shadows flit across the hill,
   The sunshine flecks the lea;
From tree to tree the robins trill
   Their songs of heartsome glee.

Where'er I go, by field or farm,
   Through grove or grassy mead,
There follows still the witching charm
   That haunts the vale of Tweed.

AT MELROSE.

The Spirit of the hoary past
   By Tweed's broad rippling flow,
To-day hath caught me firm and fast,
   And will not let me go,

But leads me on through pleasant ways,
   By wood and flowing stream;
Beneath the soft September haze,
   And Autumn's waning gleam;

And whispers softly all the way
   Of tales of other times;
That throng the paths we walk to-day,
   With pilgrims from all climes,

Who wander on by field and fell,
   Of this fair Border land;
Obedient to the potent spell
   Of the Magician's wand.

The land of legend and romance,
   Of feud and battle hot,
Of chivalry and levelled lance,
   And good Sir Walter Scott.

The home he loved beside us lies,
   World-wide its fame is made;
And Eildon's triple peaks uprise,
   Scaured by the Roman spade.

And here the Abbey's ruined walls,
   Though broken, old, and grey,
The splendour of the past recalls,
   With pathos of decay.

IN PRAISE OF TWEED.

What wealth of curious, quaint device,
   In richly carven stone,
Endures through mouldering centuries,
   While earth reclaims its own.

Oft here the master-hand recast,
   The vanished rite, and race;
While kindling fancies of the past
   Lit up his homely face.

Brave heart that bore the crushing day
   Of Fortune's dire despite,
And stoutly girded for the fray,
   Like dauntless Border knight.

Not for the love of vain applause,
   Nor eager lust of fame;
But for the high and holy cause
   That guards an honest name.

To-day the clouds grow dark and lower,
   The wind blows from the west,
In fitful gusts, as when they bore
   The Minstrel to his rest;

And left him to his lone, last sleep,
   By Dryburgh's sylvan sward;
While over all the Eildons keep
   Unwearied watch and ward.

Farewell, green vale of daring deed,
   Of song and fairy lore,
Through which the murmur of the Tweed
   Makes music evermore.

JOHN SMART, R.S.A.

Born 1838.

JOHN SMART, son of Robert Campbell Smart, was born at Edinburgh, 16th October, 1838. He was educated at the High School, Leith, and in 1851 began to study applied art at the Art School of the Hon. the Board of Trustees for Manufactures. He was apprenticed as a letter engraver in 1853; he commenced as a student with Horatio M'Culloch, the well-known landscape painter, in 1860; in 1870 he was married at Doune, in Perthshire, to Miss Agnes Purdie Main; in 1871 he was elected an A.R.S.A., and an R.S.A. in 1875. He is one of the original founders of the Royal Scottish Water Colour Society, and is also a member of the Royal Society of British Artists, London. He has received several gold medals from exhibitions in different parts of the world, and is one of the best known representatives of the Scottish school of painting. Mr Smart is also no mean adept in the art of versifying, and most of his lines have about them that cheery and breezy spirit so characteristic of his song on the Tweed.

A DAY BY THE TWEED.

There are some now who rave for a life on the wave,
    Some who rush off to Athens or Rome,
Some who spend their spare time on the banks of the Rhine,
    But for me there's more beauty near home.
So I envy them not; all such journeying's rot,
    Done in trains that dash on wi' such speed ;
And there's pleasure to me in far greater degree
    In a quiet day spent by the Tweed.

Wi' a day at "The Nest" ony man may be blest,
    Just to list to the labouring bees ;
Where the lav'rock soars high in the clear summer sky,
    And the cushat's note's borne on the breeze.
As he casts o'er the stream, just a beautiful dream,
    Or may rest a-while, puffing his weed,
O, it's certain I am, a man's not worth his dram,
    If he loves not a day by the Tweed.

Oh! I care not to stand by the Jordan's famed strand,
    If I'm banished from New Caddonlee ;
Can its beauty compare wi' the beauties o' Yair,
    Where the Tweed rushes on to the sea?
Think what pleasure we feel, up by auld Ashestiel,
    Of its beauty we'll all be agreed;
Let them sing o' the Tay, when it's smiling in May,
    But gi'e me a day by the Tweed.

For I'd rather be here, 'mang the scenes that are dear,
    By "The Peel" or oor ain Thornilee,
Than I'd trot o'er the earth, from Japan back to Perth,
    For the Tweed has mair beauty for me.
Then pardon, mine host, if I venture a toast,
    Amang fishers, of words there's no need,
"Here's to fish on the rise, of a fairly good size,
    And mair days to us a' by the Tweed."

ANDREW LANG.
Born 1844.

ANDREW LANG, one of the most versatile of modern authors, is a native of Selkirk, born 31st March, 1844, son of John Lang and Jane Plenderleath Sellar, and was educated at Edinburgh Academy, St Andrews University, and Balliol College, Oxford, where he graduated first class in classics. He is an Hon. Fellow of Merton College, Oxford; M.A. and LL.D. of St Andrews; and has been Gifford Lecturer to that University. Adopting the profession of letters, he has become one of the most prolific, and at the same time one of the brightest writers of the day. His Tweed ballads are characteristic specimens of his poetical skill, and show that, notwithstanding a life of manifolded literary activity, he has ever a warm heart to the Borderland and fair Tweedside. "Life," he writes, "is always 'the boy' when one is beside the Tweed. Times change, and we change, for the worse. But the river changes little. Still he courses through the keen and narrow rocks beneath the bridge of Yair.

> From Yair, which hills so closely bind,
> Scarce can the Tweed his passage find,
> Though much he fret, and chafe, and toil,
> Till all his eddying currents boil.

Still the water loiters by the long boat-pool of Yair, as though loath to leave the drooping boughs of the elms. Still it courses with a deep eddy through

Andrew Lang

the Elm Wheel, and ripples under Fernilea, where the author of the 'Flowers of the Forest' lived in that now mouldering and roofless hall with the peaked turrets. Still Neidpath is fair, Neidpath of the unhappy maid, and still we mark the tiny burn at Ashestiel, how in November,

> Murmuring hoarse, and frequent seen,
> Through bush and briar, no longer green,
> An angry brook, it sweeps the glade,
> Brawls over rock and wild cascade,
> And foaming brown, with doubled speed,
> Hurries its waters to the Tweed.

Still the old tower of Elibank is black and strong in ruin Elibank, the home of that Muckle-mou'd Meg, who made Harden after all a better bride than he woud have found in the hanging ash-tree of her father. These are unaltered, mainly, since the time Scott saw them last, and little altered is the homely house of Ashestiel, where he had been so happy. And we, too, feel but little change among those scenes of long ago, those best beloved haunts of boyhood, where we have had so many good days and bad, days of rising trout and success; days of failure, and even of half-drowning. One cannot reproduce the ciarm of the strong river in pool and stream, of the seep rich bank that it rushes or lingers by, of the green and heathery hills beyond, or the bare slopes where the blue slate breaks through among the dark old thorn-trees, remnants of the forest. It is all homely and all haunted, and, if a Tweedside fisher might have his desire, he would sleep the long sleep in the little churchyard that lies lonely above the pool of Caddonfoot, and hard by Christopher North's favourite quarters at Clovenfords."—*Angling Sketches*, 1891.

See also his *Ballads and Lyrics of Old France*, 1872; *Ballades in Blue China*, 1880; *Helen of Troy*, 1882; *Ballads and Verses Vain*, 1882; *Rhymes à la Mode*, 1884; *Ballads of Books*, 1888; *Grass of Parnassus*, 1888; *Ban and Arrière Ban*, 1894; *Life of John Gibson Lockhart*, 1896.—Mr Lang's edition of the *Waverley Novels*—the "Border Edition," published by Nimmo, is one of the best in the market.

TWILIGHT ON TWEED.

Three crests against the saffron sky,
   Beyond the purple plain,
The kind remembered melody
   Of Tweed once more again.

Wan water from the Border hills,
   Dear voice from the old years,
Thy distant music lulls and stills,
   And moves to quiet tears.

Like a loved ghost thy fabled flood
   Fleets through the dusky land;
Where Scott, come home to die, has stood,
   My feet returning stand.

A mist of memory broods and floats,
   The Border waters flow;
The air is full of ballad notes,
   Borne out of long ago.

Old songs that sung themselves to me,
  Sweet through a boy's day-dream,
While trout below the blossom'd tree
  Plashed in the golden stream.

. . . . .

Twilight, and Tweed, and Eildon Hill,
  Fair and too fair you be;
You tell me that the voice is still
  That should have welcomed me.

From *Ballades in Blue China.*

BALLADE OF THE TWEED.

The ferox rins in rough Loch Awe,
  A weary cry frae ony toun :
The Spey that loups o'er linn and fa',
  They praise a' ither streams aboon ;
They boast their braes o' bonny Doon :
  Gie *me* to hear the ringing reel,
Where shilfas ring and cushats croon
  By fair Tweedside, at Ashestiel !

There's Ettrick, Meggat, Ail, and a',
  Where trout swim thick in May and June,
Ye 'll see them take in showers o' snaw
  Some blisking cauldrife April noon ;
Rax ower the palmer and march-brown,
  And syne we'll show a bonny creel,
In spring or simmer, late or soon,
  By fair Tweedside, at Ashestiel !

There's mony a water, great or sma',
    Gaes ringing in his riller tune,
Through glen and heugh and hope and shaw,
    Beneath the sunlicht or the moon ;
But set us in our fishing shoon
    Between the Caddon burn and Peel,
And syne we'll cross the heather broun
    By fair Tweedside, at Ashestiel !

ENVOY.

Deil tak the dirty trading loon
    Wad gar his water ca' his wheel,
And drift his dyes and poisons down
    By fair Tweedside, at Ashestiel !

From *Ballades in Blue China.*

APRIL ON TWEED.

As birds are fain to build their nest
    The first soft sunny day,
So longing wakens in my breast
    A month before the May.
When now the wind is from the West
    And Winter melts away.

The snow lies yet on Eildon Hill,
    But soft the breezes blow,
Of melting snows the waters fill,
    We nothing heed the snow ;
But we must up and take our will,—
    A-fishing we will go.

IN PRAISE OF TWEED.

Below the branches brown and bare,
  Beneath the primrose lea,
The trout lies waiting for his fare,
  A hungry trout is he;
He's hooked, and springs and splashes there
  Like salmon from the sea!

Oh, April tide's a pleasant tide,
  However times may fall,
And sweet to welcome Spring, the Bride,
  You hear the mavis call;
But all adown the waterside
  The Spring's most fair of all.

From *Grass of Parnassus*.

ALEXANDER ANDERSON
("SURFACEMAN.")

BORN 1845.

ALEXANDER ANDERSON, one of the best-known and beloved of living Scottish poets, was born on 30th April, 1845, at Kirkconnel, in the county of Dumfries. His boyhood was spent at the Galloway hamlet of Crocketford, where he received his early education. For a considerable number of years he worked on the railway as a surfaceman, hence the new name, "Surfaceman," bestowed upon him by the muse, which has supplanted his own name as completely as "The Ettrick Shepherd" that of James Hogg, or "Hildebrand" that of the genial Hollander, Nicolaus Beets. Latterly, Mr Anderson has acted as one of the Librarians in the University of Edinburgh. He is a true poet, and though he would be the first to admit that he does not stand in the front rank, yet he is a great poet also. He has sought his themes in many places, and with hardly less truth than in its original application, it may be said of him, "Whatever he has touched he has adorned." His poems on graver subjects have successfully undergone the criticism of the highest; they have had an appreciative welcome from our best literary guides—men like Gilfillan and Saintsbury. But the public also—the great mass of the Scottish people—are wonderful critics in their way, and their word has most cordially seconded the voices of their literary superiors. Of course, Mr Anderson has also written pieces which more specially appeal to them. It is questionable if anything so sweet and yet so simple as "Cuddle Doon" has ever appeared in the Scottish tongue since Burns's "To a mountain Daisy." Of Mr Anderson, more than of any Scottish poet of the present day, it may truly be said that there is something distinct and distinguished about every line he writes; not that he does not sometimes fall below the standard which he himself has created, but even in such places we can trace the unmistakeable mark of the true 'maker.' In the lines on the Tweed given below, we discover the poet in one of his most sympathetic humours, manifesting that feeling for the world around him which recalls Wordsworth in his best moods, and that glamour over the past which speaks of the matchless Wizard, whose magic he so lovingly celebrates. Mr Anderson has published the following volumes of verse:—

A Song of Labour and Other Poems, 1873. "Advertiser" Office, Dundee.

The Two Angels and Other Poems, 1875. Simpkin, Marshall, & Co.

Songs of the Rail, 1878. Simpkin, Marshall, & Co.

Ballads and Sonnets, 1879. Macmillan, London.

WHEN FIRST I SAW THE TWEED.

When first I saw the Tweed, the light
    Of autumn, tender, sad and grey,
Lay on the Eildon's triple height,
    And lent a sadness to the day.

It fell on field and wood around,
    Soft as a single leaf may fall;
It mingled with the river's sound,
    And gave a meaning unto all.

And, as I slowly walked, I felt
    An unseen presence step with me,
That gave to field and woodland belt
    A universal memory.

I heard the Tweed, but in its voice
    That came to me, another rang;
I lent myself to dreams by choice—
    I knew the mighty minstrel sang.

And, lo, as at a trumpet call,
    I saw knights, grim of look, and bold,
Crash through the lists, or, dying, fall
    Within their harness as of old;

I saw the royal pageant glide
    In floods of plume and pennons gay,
And barons in their armour'd pride,
    And silken ladies, glad and gay;

Grim warders on each border keep,
    To cry the foray when it nears:—
I saw the rough-clad troopers sweep
    The moonlight gleaming on their spears.

All this, as in a mirror, pass'd,
 A dim old world of sunken things,
To waken, as it did at last,
 When one great Wizard touch'd the strings.

He sleeps beside the Tweed to-day,
 Whose music mingles with his dream;
And this is why my footsteps stray,
 And why I linger by the stream.

Thou river of the minstrel's heart,
 Whose latest murmur reach'd his ear,
Thou soundest, as though far apart,—
 His only is the voice I hear.

Flow, then, around his sacred dust,
 Through the long years that are to be,
And leave the Eildons to their trust,
 To sentinel his memory.

"EFFIE."

Born 1846.

"Effie" Williamson, or Mrs Gavin Dickson, of Romanno Bridge, Peeblesshire, has been long known in Border circles as a poetess of no mean merit. Born at Galashiels, 29th March, 1846, she was sent, very early in life, to work in one of the large woollen factories of the district. In 1868 her father removed to Ireland as manager of the Blarney Mills, near Cork, and a few years' residence in the Emerald Isle did much to strengthen the character, and mould the poetic tastes of his gifted daughter. "Effie" looks back to this time with unbounded pleasure, notwithstanding the fact that her Irish sojourn was just when the Fenian agitation was at its height, and the family had on one occasion to experience a 'boycott' long before that word had been associated with its modern meaning. From Ireland they returned to Gala Water and the banks of Tweed, where "Effie" resumed her old occupation at the loom. In 1883 the *Tangled Web* was published, and a large edition went out of print within a few months. Mr Gladstone wrote kindly of her little volume to the young authoress, a copy of which had been forwarded to him, and in return he presented her with a book from his own library. *Peaceable Fruits*—a dainty collection of sacred poems, con-

Alexander Brown.

John Smart

Alexander Anderson.

J. Logie Robertson.

tributed chiefly to English magazines, was issued in 1885, and has proved an inspiring influence to many readers. In 1889 " Effie " was married, and her life has since been spent amid the quiet uplands of Peeblesshire, in one of its most charming parishes.

See *The Border Counties Magazine*, Galashiels, May 1881, and *The Border Magazine*, Glasgow, vol. 1, November 1896.

A SUMMER DAY'S DRIVE.

Queen Autumn, lovely in decay,
Hath donned once more her bright array
   Of gold and brown; o'er hill and down,
In pensive mood, at twilight's fall,
Sad memory lingers to recall
      The Summer flown,
Its joys still claiming as her own.

Outstanding clear; a fresh delight,
One day above all others bright
   Awakes to view. O memory true
To inward promptings of my heart,
Lend me but words to do my part,
      The poet's pen
To paint hill, vale, and wooded glen!

Each murmuring stream from Lyne to Tweed,
The sunlit hills and flowery mead,
   Past which we sped, as fancy led,

IN PRAISE OF TWEED.

That summer day, my friend and I;
Heart spoke to heart, and eye to eye,
    With beaming glance:
Our happy spirits in a trance.

Of gladness words were vain to tell;
Each felt the power of Nature's spell,
    As in a dream; yon babbling stream,
That, singing, rushes to its rest
At last on Tweed's calm flowing breast,
    The emblem meet
Of joy in silent bliss complete.

E'en so with us, friend, by-and-bye,
Our merry laughter seemed to die
    In deeper bliss. Ah! was not this
Of Summer's gifts the brightest day?
Dear friend of mine, though far away,
    Our hearts unite
In this sweet gift of memory bright.

And still I doubt not as you read,
You see the Lyne flow down to Tweed,
    Its sunny way, past castle grey;
And breezy hills, outstanding fair,
Feel once again the balmy air
    O'er moor and fen;
Yet stay, sweet memory, stay my pen,

Unskilled in art, lest it should wrong
The silver Tweed, renowned in song.
    Enchanted stream, where poets dream,
We, too, in humble homage bend,
As up its wooded vales we wend
    Our homeward way,
Beneath the sunset's golden ray.

SPRING BY TWEEDSIDE.

Come, Willie, back to Tweed's fair stream,
Not now, 'neath chill November's gleam
   The fallen leaves lie dying;
Cold Winter's gone, and through the wood
The balmy winds in genial mood
   Of Summer days are sighing.

Sweet Spring o'er valley, hill, and dell,
Has come with soft, bewitching spell,
   To wake all beauties sleeping;
The fresh, green leaves come out to see,
And lo! from under bush and tree,
   The primrose, shyly peeping.

Bright buttercups unfurl their gold;
From grassy sward, half shy, half bold,
   See daisy eyes up-glancing;
And down in yonder sheltered glade,
All in their nodding plumes arrayed,
   Wild hyacinths are dancing.

'Neath fern and moss, half hid from view,
The violet opes her eyes of blue,
   Their beauty rare revealing;
O'er scraggy banks the wild woodbine
With trailing sprays of ivy twine,
   The rugged rock concealing.

Flower, brook, and bird, new life receive;
From early morn till dewy eve
   What babbling and what singing!
Through leafy boughs the notes prolong,
Where flit glad birds with cheerful song
   On love's fond errand winging.

IN PRAISE OF TWEED.

    Come, Willie, haste thee back with speed,
    And see the winding banks of Tweed,
       In Summer dress beguiling.
    O'er all the world where you have been
    Say, Willie, have you ever seen
       A land so fair and smiling?

From *The Tangled Web*.

JAMES LOGIE ROBERTSON.

("HUGH HALIBURTON.")

BORN 1846.

JAMES LOGIE ROBERTSON, M.A. ("Hugh Haliburton"), born at Milnathort, Kinross-shire, 18th September, 1846; educated at Orwell Parish School and Edinburgh University, where he greatly distinguished himself in the classes of English Literature and Geology. He was appointed to, but declined the Professorship of Humanity in Adrian College, Michigan, U.S.A. He is now First English Master, Edinburgh Ladies' College. He is one of the best writers of modern vernacular poetry, and has published the following:—

Poems. John Leng & Co., Dundee, 1878.
Orellana and other Poems, 1881.
Our Holiday among the Hills, 1882.
Horace in Homespun, 1886.
Ochil Idylls, 1891.
Dunbar To-day—Adaptations from Dunbar, 1895.

See also his prose essays :

For Puir Auld Scotland's Sake, 1887.
In Scottish Fields, 1890.
Furth in Field, 1894.

SUMMER GLOAMING ON TWEEDSIDE.

Now what is this charm that's a-weaving,
    That stirs in my pulse and my hair?
Is it an angel that's cleaving
    The deeps of the darkening air?

There's a spell on the hour! Ah! the *new* moon!
    (How *did* she get into the sky?)
So shyly her splendour assuming! . . . .
    That was a bat that flew by.

There's peace in the dome of heaven's temple;
    The pulse of the air is at rest;
The pool shows no longer a dimple;
    The blue dove moans on her nest.

There! caught in the calm of the gloaming—
    Whence came the enchantment I see?
Is it a maid that was roaming,
    Took fright, and was changed to a tree?

In leaf and in twig she is hearkening;
    She is holding her breath lest I hear!
Still deepens between us the darkening,
    Till—now she escapes with her fear!

From *Ochil Idylls*, where it is entitled "Summer Gloaming in Gleneagles." The lines, however, as the author writes, were originally written on a Tweedside gloaming.

THE TWEED.

"And this is the Tweed—the glorious river of Scottish romance!—whose steel-clear waters make once more their melody in our ears. Not *that* the mere sound of sliding waters, such as the love-lorn wanderer hears crying through the wilderness of the New World. It is the voice of Eld, conning over, with total disregard of the present, its many waning memories. There is a sadness in the tone, which the river has caught from its long and intimate association with vanished man. All the voices of Nature are originally cheerful; where they are tinged with melancholy man has been there to change the key, and disarrange the primal harmony. And well, O Tweed, may thy song sound in our hearing with something of the character of a lament; for thou, for many a century bygone, hast witnessed alike the oft-repeated follies of human passion and the transitoriness of earthly renown! Where now the moonlighted moss-trooper of the old Border days?—the men-at-arms, the mail-clad knights of the age of chivalry, who have spurred along thy banks, time-hallowed river—who have swum on errand of love or war thy tranquil waters, or, it may be, have mingled their life-stream with thine? The heedless river keeps on its unintelligible murmur; it will not share its secrets."

From "A Holiday in Arcadia," in *For Puir Auld Scotland's Sake.*

THE REV. JOHN BUCHAN.

BORN 1847.

THE REV. JOHN BUCHAN was born at Peebles in 1847. He received his education there and at Edinburgh University. In 1874 he was ordained to the ministry of the Free Church of Scotland at Perth, and is now minister of John Knox's Church, Glasgow. In 1881 he issued a small volume of much poetical merit, entitled "Tweedside Echoes and Moorland Musings."[1] He is an earnest and eloquent preacher, a diligent pastor, and a man of singularly attractive qualities. His son is the well-known author of *Sir Quixote of the Moors, Scholar Gipsies, Musa Piscatrix, John Burnet of Barns, Grey Weather*, etc.

[1][Edinburgh: John Maclaren & Sons.]

THE TWEED.

A moorland well, half-hid by rushes green,
Fringed with forget-me-not and meadow-bloom,
Parent of tiny stream that maketh room
Among the reedy grass; its glistening sheen
Now seen, now lost behind the flowery screen;
Nourished by rill and rain and misty gloom,
A thing of power, its gathering waters loom
Through summer haze, across the upland scene.

Flow on, fair stream, by bush and bank and scaur,
By haunted tower, or ancient burgh town;
Linked to thy wave are tales of love and war,
And deeds of chivalry by dale and down,
Hail, queen of Border rivers! thine the star,
The silver sceptre, and the crystal crown.

From *Tweedside Echoes*.

TWEED AND YARROW.

O silver Tweed! that floweth soft
  Where willows weep and aspens quiver;
How sweet the music of thy wave,
  Thou sparkling pleasant-winding river!

Thy liquid lapse by tower and town,
  In every varying phase and measure,
Aye singing to an olden tune
  Thy song of ancient love and pleasure.

The lilt of birds, the scent of flowers,
  Beneath the tangled woody cover,
Where shepherd swains at noon repose,
  And modest maiden meets her lover.

Thy stream seems always lit with smiles,
  And ne'er grows dark and drumlie water;
The pipe and reed thy music sweet,
  And not the bugle breathing slaughter.

Far other 't is with yon lone stream,
  Though bright its course when morning shineth,
And sweetly mirrored in its wave
  The pale moon's gleam when eve declineth.

By birken bower and dowie den,
  Where'er thou flowest, rueful Yarrow,
A melancholy moan thy wave,
  An undertone of deathless sorrow.

The "gentle wind that bloweth south"
  Breathes o'er the grave of slaughtered lover,
And ever o'er this woeful vale
  A weeping spirit seems to hover.

And yet thou meet'st the silver Tweed,
  And pleasure sweet is wed to sorrow ;
True emblem of our changeful life,
  Till o'er us break a brighter morrow.

From *Tweedside Echoes.*

AN AUTUMN THOUGHT.

How clear thy waters, silver Tweed !
  How sweet their melody !
By tower and town and verdant down
  E'en to the flowing sea.

But clearer far the flood of life
  Pours forth its crystal stream ;
And sweeter far its melody,
  Where jasper turrets gleam.

Slow-waning Neidpath's leafy wood,
  Pale autumn o'er it cast ;
Tweed's stream will soon be foaming rude
  Beneath the winter's blast.

On life's translucent stream, no storm
A wavelet stirs, I ween;
And in the fair green tree of life
No autumn leaf is seen.

From *Tweedside Echoes*.

VOICES OF THE TWEED.

As I lay listening to the waters deep
That ever laved the rock beneath my feet,
Like dream-shapes when the eyes are weigh'd with sleep,
Voices arose, blent in a murmur sweet—
The sigh of Prophet Merlin, as he wept
By the green mound which men now call his grave;
The tramp of heroes who their fealty kept,
And quell'd the Southron by the Esk's clear wave;
A flying reiver's hoofs, the heath that spurn,
In fiery haste along the mountain side;
The breeze-borne note of psalm beside the burn
Where hunted worshippers were forced to hide;
And eke thy love-lay Yester, all forlorn,
The wandering victim of a maiden's scorn.

From *Tweedside Echoes*.

TWEEDSMUIR.

No splintered peaks of granite cleave the blue,
   But soft round masses flowing wave on wave,
A swelling sea far as the eye can view,
   Mouldings of nature, emerald in hue,
Where misty vapours shroud the Cymric grave,
   Last resting-place of those whom Saxons slew,

As pressing northward still, they stronger grew,
   And dispossessed the pristine dwellers brave.
O sweet sun-smitten summits! smooth and green,
   What secrets have ye which in vain we crave:
Merlin and Kentigern ye knew, I ween;
   And ever as your sides Tweed's waters lave,
Their weird-like forms still float before the eye,
   Dim visions of a hoar antiquity.

From *Tweedside Echoes*.

NEIDPATH AT EVENTIDE.

The gloamin' grey is gathering fast
   Ower Neidpath's grassy braes;
The e'enin' win' wi' soughin' soun'
   Amang the woodland plays.

Sweet murm'rin' in their rocky bed,
   Tweed's siller waters flow;
To kiss the ripple o' the tide
   The saughs are bendin' low.

Frae yonder covert o' green firs
   Is heard the cushat's note;
And ower the calm which naething stirs,
   The love-notes gently float.

The sun has westered ower the hill,
   The length'nin' shadows fa';
But glints o' glory linger roun'
   The crumblin' castle wa'.

A dewy calm is settlin' doun
  Upon the earth's green breast,
Soft as a mother's kiss that soothes
  Her infant to its rest.

Sweet change frae witherin' heat o' day,
  The dewy e'enin' calm;
It comes to bush and flower and tree—
  Kind nature's healin' balm.

May peace distil on ilka heart,
  Like dew upon the blade;
And may the weary rest secure
  In Israel's Keeper's shade!

From *Tweedside Echoes*.

JAMES LOGIE HERCUS.
1847-1885.

JAMES LOGIE HERCUS was born at Kirkwall, and educated at the Grammar School of the Orcadian Capital. Removing southwards, he spent some years of commercial activity in Edinburgh, and latterly in Glasgow, where he died in 1885. A small volume—"Songs of the Borderland and other Verses," was issued from the press of J. & J. H. Rutherfurd of Kelso, in 1888, under the editorship of W. A. Clouston, editor of *Arabian Poetry for English Readers*, &c. Writing of the author, he says, " Mr Hercus was content to sing, in humble but pleasing strains, the praises of the Scottish Borderland, already so famed in song and story; and occasionally to give expression in verse (which, if not always faultless in construction, is never without 'the stamp and clear impression of good sense') to his reflections on a number of subjects which are of universal interest to humanity. He decidedly possessed much of the true poet's appreciation of the charms of Nature. Many of his pieces evince a pleasing melancholy, while others have an invigorating swing, and are full of martial fire and patriotic fervour. His productions entitle him to remembrance as one of our gifted bards."

THE TWEED.

Thou classic stream, the world-renowned,
    Wherever Scotsmen roam—
Round thee the exile's mem'ry twines,
    In lands beyond the foam!
Stream of our glorious fatherland,
    That, ever rushing free,
Through fairy groves and green alcoves,
    Meanders to the sea.

Wide through the classic Borderland
    Rolls on thy limpid wave,
By castled tower and donjon keep,
    Where prostrate lies the brave;
Bright be thy wanderings in the glade,
    Through flowery mead and lea;
Then roll along, with murmuring song,
    Thy waters to the sea.

Full many an ancient field of fight
    Is by thy waters laved;
Where erst o'er Scotia's warlike ranks
    Her ruddy line has waved.
Then roll along, by tower and town,
    Thy waters to the sea;
And as thou flows, o'er ancient foes,
    Sing pæans to the free.

Thou fairest river of our land,
    That classic poets sang,
And o'er whose wave the trembling harp
    Of mystic Merlin rang;
Beloved thy every sweep and turn,
    Renowned in minstrelsy,
Through flowery glades, 'neath green arcades,
    Meander to the sea.

From *Songs of the Borderland.*

DUNCAN FRASER.

Born 1848.

Duncan Fraser is a native of Edinburgh, where he is a teacher of music, and holds several important public appointments, amongst others that of precentor to the General Assembly of the Free Church. He is a Fellow of various educational and musical societies, and has written extensively on musical and cognate subjects. A lover of nature and a keen angler, he spends most of his holiday hours in the pursuit of his favourite pastime.

See his *Riverside Rambles of an Edinburgh Angler*—Selkirk: George Lewis & Co. (1896).

AN ANGLER'S RHAPSODY.

The soul-inspiring Tweed! Surely never did one set himself a more difficult task than when he resolved to sing the praises of this enchanting river.

Poets, from the earliest times have caught the tones of its swirling current, and striven to re-echo them on lyres of many varying strings.

Painters have revelled amid the manifold beauty that engirdles it from its source 'mong silent hills in pastoral Tweedsmuir, to its outflow in the stormy northern sea.

"Effie."

Rev. John Buchan.

J. L. Hercus.

Duncan Fraser

Historians have as yet failed to exhaust the wealth of national incident that had for its arena the debatable land through which this classic river flows.

But if you would understand how it comes that the very name of a stream can enthrall mankind, just mention the word " Tweed " in the hearing of one who has enrolled himself under the banner of the genial, poetic, stream-loving Izaak Walton! We care not though the season be marked by winter's sternest frown — with days but short and joys but few : nor matters it that time has thinned the erstwhile raven locks, or taken the elasticity from the limbs so vigorous in bygone days : once an angler, always an angler!

And so, at the sound of the name of that river, endeared by associations that shall endure while memory lasts, the old angler forgets his present surroundings—his eye gleams and his pulse quickens—his form is drawn up to its full height, and his hand works firmly from the wrist in a peculiar way; at the same time, he becomes conscious of the blood coursing through his veins as if it had become suddenly charged with the elixir of life ; in short, he has shed his threescore years and ten, and stands before you re-juvenated—a youth once more!

In fancy our friend is wafted away to the river of his first love; the sun is shining—it always shone in those days—the birds are in full song, and singing as they never sing now; the hills are flushed with purpling heather, while the fields and verdant riverbanks are gay with flowers as countless as they are varied.

To his fancy the wind set ever in the south at that halcyon time, and skies bore only clouds sufficient to temper the glare of the sun at noonday! Tweed knew no drought, but ran ever full and amber-coloured, while pollution and its attendant mysteries were unknown and undreamed of! (Ah, he is a visionary indeed!) There lies the nut-wood pool, and yonder flows the swirling gurly!—But stay, who does not know how the old soldier

> Shouldered his crutch
> And showed how fields were won?

And so we leave the scene to be finished according to the imagination of each reader, for words would fail to describe the reminiscent deeds of a veteran angler, when the thought of Tweedside has bridged for him years of pain and sorrow!

A MEMORY.

A "first day" on the Tweed! recall it not,
    Else all around will stale and sombre grow;
A first day on the Tweed! what joy it brought,
    When life was young, and hope's rose tints did glow.

The music of the river wrought a spell entrancing
  Around the hearts of lingerers by its shore;
The ripples on the waves in sunlight dancing,
  Memory can ne'er efface till life's dream is o'er.

The thrill of Spring's return, 'mid song of blithe birds,
  Made pulses throb, and eyes with gladness burn;
The verdant banks, with gowans glinting heavenwards,
  Smiled, as if in joy to herald our return.

Unchanged all seemed to fond imagination,
  Since last we trod the gem-bespangled lea;
The cuckoo and the lapwing swelled the diapason
  Which grateful nature sent aloft from field and tree.

We carried in our hearts a song that morning,
  Which echoed back from vale, and stream, and brae:
Would that our lives, fell Fortune's buffets scorning,
  Could keep the faith we sang in life's first day!

From *Riverside Rambles of an Edinburgh Angler.*

WILLIAM SANDERSON.

BORN 1852.

WILLIAM SANDERSON ("Tweedside Laddie") is a native of Edinburgh, but claims to be, and is most of all, a Borderer by family descent, residence, and personal attachment. His early days were spent at Innerleithen, of which town his parents were natives, and where, no doubt, the associations of the district "kindled his poetic fire." After a brief residence in London, he spent some years in his Tweedside home, and is now manager of a well-known musical firm in Glasgow. He has been a constant contributor, chiefly on Border subjects, to the provincial press; and several of his songs, wedded to appropriate melody by himself, have been published, and are deservedly popular.

A DREAM OF TWEED.

A SONG OF BORDERLAND.

Dear Borderland of classic streams,
Sweet Borderland of poets' dreams,
Brave Borderland of sons so free,
The Borderland's the land for me!

IN PRAISE OF TWEED.

When far from home I dream of Tweed,
   And peace comes to me in my dream,
I see once more the grassy mead,
   And hear the murmur of the stream.
I watch the crystal water glide,
   I mark the pebbles on the strand,
The sedge blades quiv'ring in thy tide,
   Dear river of the Borderland.

From green Tweed's Well thy course I trace,
   Past Neidpath grey to Ashestiel;
Who marks not all thy wondrous grace,
   A caitiff he who cannot feel—
For mem'ry strikes a magic chord,
   And beauty leads to beauties rare;
Till Tweed flows on by Abbotsford.
   And Melrose rears her ruin fair.

The bending alders kiss the wave,
   And cast a leafy shadow cool,
While round the rocks the waters lave,
   Where lurk the troutlets in the pool.
The pool whose bosom mirrors still
   The ruined peel and ivied tower,
While lending force to yonder mill
   That turns obedient to its power.

One after one, in colours bright,
   The scenes familiar pass along,
While in the visions of the night
   I hear the strains of Border song.
At old Traquair there's peaceful calm,
   And Leithen vale is fair indeed;
O'er scene and song floats Nature's psalm—
   The gentle murmurs of the Tweed

Where Kelso's wooded islets rise
    To grace the wedded rivers twain,
I watch thy tide with raptured eyes
    Flow calmly through the flow'ry plain.
I feel the breezes fan my cheek,
    As by some scaur I take my stand,
And as they pass I hear them speak
    Of thee, my own dear Borderland.

By verdant haughs and heath-clad hills,
    Our river flows both deep and wide,
Fed by a hundred sparkling rills
    And classic streams that swell its tide.
Then where old Berwick proudly stands
    And braves the North Sea's fiercest blast,
The pride of all the Border lands
    Glides into Ocean's arms at last.

'T is but a dream, and yet perchance
    My spirit wings its wayward flight,
Released by sleep's mysterious trance
    To wander through the realms of night.
But spirit flight or mem'ry's dream,
    It matters not—so I may stand
Once more beside thy crystal stream,
    Dear river of my Fatherland.

NAE WUNNER TWEED'S REMEMBERED.

Nae wunner Tweed's remembered—there's music in the name
That gars the heart forget itsel' when far awa' frae hame;
That drives awa' life's sma' annoys and bids oor sorrows flee,
As lifts the mist frae yon brae-face when wind blaws frae the sea.

Ye 'll meet wi' streams mair lordly far, in distant foreign lands,
That row 'mang scenes majestical or flow through gowden sands;
Yet, while ye 're lost in wonderment, the heart tak's little heed—
It wadna change for a' the gowd ae pebble frae the Tweed.

There 's something in the silver Tweed we canna weel explain,
That thrills each heart that e'er has dwelt on Border hill or plain;
That seems to tell us wondrous tales o' days when time was young,
And croons the weel-lo'ed accents ower o' oor soft Lowland tongue.

Ay! weel may Tweed remembered be, for ilka rock and stream
Has some auld warld tale to tell that haunts us like a dream,
And brings to mind each bonnie spot frae Tweedsmuir to the sea—
To such a stream whaur is the heart that wadna loyal be?

WILLIAM CUTHBERTSON.

BORN 1857.

WILLIAM CUTHBERTSON was born at Edinburgh, 21st May, 1857. His early years were spent in the ancient and historic town of Berwick-on-Tweed, and thus his furthest-back memories are associated with the noble river, which there mingles with the sea. It was again, however, to Edinburgh that he went for his education and his business training; and though treasuring his associations of the past, he has now become quite identified with the active life—in every sense—of the Capital. The head of an extensive and flourishing business, he has yet found opportunity to make himself useful to his fellow-citizens in divers manners. He now acts as Secretary of the honourable body of the Edinburgh High Constables. In association with Professor Patrick Geddes, he has successfully tried his hand at brightening the environment of many a shadowed life, and letting God's sunlight shine into many a dark corner. As a pilot of the National Home Reading Union, he has guided many a party of excursionists through the beauties of the Pentlands; and many a village charity has found in him an active and energetic helper. But even all this does not exhaust the innate energy of the man. Those who know him can testify to his love of the muse, and his appreciation of the creations of others. He is never more at home than when he is in the country, gazing on nature's fairest scenes, and weaving his thoughts, touched by the ceaseless charms of the world around him, into glowing verse and ringing rhyme. No land is dearer to him than the Scottish Borderland and "Tweed's fair river broad and deep." Tweed is ever making an appeal to his poetic fancy. She is that thing of beauty which is a joy for ever. Along her broad, clear, and sinuous course, the worries of business fade into a dim and formless background of haze, while the beauties around call forth a deep emotional response. Such a response finds its truest æsthetical expression in poetry. The overflow of delight is distinctly rhythmic, though it may not be said that every one "lisps in numbers." The verses on "Berwick Bay" will show that our bard is no mean disciple of the famous muse, and he has published, though not yet in book form, many proofs of his poetic skill. He is a frequent contributor to the columns of *The Scotsman*, *Life and Work*, and other newspapers and magazines.

BERWICK BAY.

I see once more the good old town,
   I linger near each well-known scene,
And watch the shadows creeping down
   The old-world streets and lanes between.

IN PRAISE OF TWEED.

Near each loved spot I stray till night
    Has drawn her mantle o'er the day,
For there is music in the sight
    Of twinkling lights in Berwick Bay.

Under the ramparts, near the stream
    Whereon the waves moan ceaselessly,
I seem to hear, as in a dream,
    Tweed's kisses as she meets the sea;
Blue skies profound bend soft and reach
    A sea as blue, whose muffled tune
Comes softly from the farther beach,
    And breaks the slumbrous peace of noon

Sweet memories of youth's swift day
    Come crowding with the tinkling fall
Of waters, as they softly play
    And waken echoes musical.
For youth flies fast on Hermes' wing,
    And dies long years before 't is still—
Ah! dear dead days. Ah! happy spring.
    Oh! honey of Hymettus Hill.

The ghosts of bygone years that glean
    The present peace, and only come
To murmur of what might have been;
    This slumbrous hour now holds them dumb.
I've sought the shade of unknown trees
    On Europe's soil, 'neath Simla's sun;
I've pierced the waste of western seas,
    And now my feet are homeward come.

The yellow flood still flows anear
    The Lorelei and Drachenfels
That murmured in the poet's ear,
    And wove the magic of his spells.

From Spires to Köln 't is sweet to stray,
  Castle and vineyards charm the sight,
But sweeter far to me the way
  Tweed winds to seek the ocean bright.

Through leagues of wood and prairie free
  Full far and fleet Mackenzie pours
His torrents to the silent sea
  That laves the far-off Arctic shores.
Through varying scenes of field and fell,
  Majestic rolls his volumes down;
Ah! sweeter is the mead and dell,
  Tweed seeks to greet her Border town.

When night has whispered to the snow
  That hides the Himalayan crest,
The Milky Way shines out as though
  It showed the pathway of the blest.
That radiant path of heaven is bright
  O'er Simla's hills that sheds its ray,
But there is magic in the sight
  Of twinkling lights in Berwick Bay.

DRYBURGH.

The western splendour fades into the night,
  And faint winds steal upon the Cowdenknowes;
The purple Eildons wear a fringe of light
  Upon their distant brows.

Down in the valley where the river sighs
  Rippling and murmuring o'er its shallow bed,
Ghostly and cold the grey mists softly rise,
  Ere yet the eve is dead.

And like to spectres, ghostly, wan and pale,
  They swathe the ruins and the yew-tree glade ;
The cloistered calm lists to the river's wail,
  That mourns the Wizard's shade.

And though his bones have mingled with the dust,
  His words have stirred the souls of men to-day ;
The transient beauty of this evening must
  Forgotten pass away.

The last rose flush of dusky eve has fled,
  And o'er the world a leaden sceptre lies,
Another day is gathered to the dead,
  And here are darkened skies.

Power dies and beauty passes, we who dwell
  On evanescent glories mourn their end ;
The pregnant words of searchers at Truth's well,
  The roll of Time transcend.

ANON.

1859.

THE song that follows is taken from *Scottish Ballads and Songs*, edited by James Maidment, Edinburgh: T. G. Stevenson (1859). It was printed originally in the "Border Miscellany," of which one number only appeared, some years since—the publisher, Walter Thomson, having emigrated to America. He claimed, in the female line, a descent from the family of Lindsay. The song is said to have been taken from an unpublished opera called *Odonto*, or "The Murder of the Miller's Fields."

THE SILVER TWEED.

I've traversed many pleasant lands,
    I've wandered far and near;
I've sailed upon the glorious Rhine,
    And sat by Windermere;
But no place that I ever saw,
    In beauty can exceed
The fruitful fields, and waving woods,
    That bound the silver Tweed.

IN PRAISE OF TWEED.

The moon, that placid orb of night,
   Moves on in majesty,
And softens with her liquid light
   The azure of the sky ;
Her beams illume the distant hills,
   And fall upon the mead,
And quivering, dance like fairy elves,
   Upon the silver Tweed.

How sweet and soothing is the scene!
   The soft and gentle wind
Dispels those vapours of the brain
   That irritate the mind ;
And discontent, and all the cares
   That angry passions feed,
Evanish when my thoughts recall
   The beauties of the Tweed.

From Maidment's *Scottish Ballads and Songs.*

JAMES MABON.

Born 1862.

James Mabon is a native of Ancrum, Roxburghshire, and is now employed as a commercial clerk in Galashiels. For many years he has been a regular contributor to newspaper and magazine literature, writing under various signatures. In 1895 he published *Rose and Thorn*, a collection of his poetical effusions, which was very favourably received; and in 1897 he issued a second selection of poems and short prose pictures under the title of *Shingle and Sand*, which has also been heartily taken up. Mr Mabon's poetry is characterised by deep sympathy for Nature in her many moods, and the ability to depict with rare fidelity Nature as she manifests herself with such bewitching beauty along Tweedside and by the banks of Yarrow and Ettrick.

TWEED AND YARROW:
A MAY DUET.

Tweed blithely sings her seaward song,
  Where Neidpath woods grow fair,
With mosses sweet about their feet
  And hawthorn in their hair.

But valour casts a tender glance,
  Where love is lying low,
And blends the songs of knightly wrongs
  With Yarrow's silver flow.

Too softly sad your Yarrow glides
  Beside each still green brae;
The singer hears the fall of tears
  In all her pensive lay.

But sweetly sings the Shepherd's bird
  Above each fragrant mead!
Ah! you should hear the blackbird's clear
  Fond piping on the Tweed,

Where sun and shadow fleck the fields
  And blooms nod in the grass;
Your hills but lie calm 'neath the sky,
  To watch the white clouds pass.

Nay! Silence, Sorrow's sister, here
  Weaves peace both noon and night—
Such peace as lays, for other days,
  Love's dead face in our sight!

I'll sing my Yarrow, thou thy Tweed,
  So love to love shall draw;
While sunbeams play on Newark grey,
  Or sleep on Bowerhope Law.

Sing thou thy Yarrow, gentle soul,
  Tweed still must be my care,
While summer dreams in golden gleams
  Slant o'er the hills of Yair.

TWILIGHT ON TWEED.

Dreaming where the wild rose blows
  On the dewy breast of June,
Where the sleepy river flows
  'Neath the shadow of a moon.

WILLIAM CUTHBERTSON.

WILLIAM SANDERSON.

JAMES MABON.

W. S. CROCKETT.

Where the sigh of virgin night,
  Through the dusky chambers borne,
Borrows odorous delight
  From the snow-white woodland thorn.

Where the spirit of a lay
  Never will its secret give,
Moving on the grassy way,
  Song for ever fugitive.

Where a truce divine is laid
  Over weary heart and brain;
Like the stillness of the shade,
  Gifting earth with silver rain.

Fragrant earth, what bliss is mine;
  Rose at rest, sweet heart of June;
River, where the pale stars shine
  With the shadow of a moon.

Sweet, too sweet, is all this bliss,
  Hearts for very joy might weep,
Where in dreams of tenderness
  Love itself is laid asleep.

All too near at times thou art:
  For the spirit in me leans
To the beating of the heart
  Where the thin veil intervenes.

While the soul of summer sweet,
  Brooding o'er the sleeping land,
Hushes din of careless feet
  With the lifting of a hand.

From *Rose and Thorn*.

SPRING-TIDE ON TWEED.

The sweets of morn, on every side the bliss
   Of pulsing life fresh from the rest of night,
The fields of green, the early blooms, the kiss
   Of wandering winds with odorous delight,
Proclaiming now the birth of jocund Spring,
When hearts can hope and hoping gladly sing.

By verdant meads fair Tweed now softly glides
   In joyous mood—as in the years long gone,
And to its grassy margin still confides
   The sacred sweetness of a chastened tone;
Whispers, perchance, how, smiling to the blue,
Its rapturous gaze has won a kindred hue.

Now while the birds with jubilate thrill
   The greenwood aisle, earth gifts again her best
In leaf and flower, and triumph song to fill
   The open spirit of a stranger guest,
Who seeks her palace, wondering as he wends
His triumph way—where love begins and ends.

The mighty minstrel of the golden day
   Of high romance here dreamed his glorious art,
Knit lands together in his tender lay
   And charmed the shadow from a nation's heart,
Fought sorrow's self in that all-hallowed past,
And here sought home to fall asleep at last.

Now sylvan spirits waking from repose
   Weave Tweed's gay glamour with old Time's refrain;
While wild birds sing, and bursting buds disclose
   A deeper mystery than bard can gain;
Life rings with joy, and love alone is lord,
Where Spring dawns in the vales of Abbotsford.

THE VALLEY PATH.

I took the valley path to-day
    That wanders through the meadow
Where waters dimple, blue and grey
    About the alder shadow.

And there were voices in the wood,
    And songs upon the river;
An interchange of mood with mood
    That rhymed about me ever.

Star blossoms gazed, and left and right
    Were tender ivies clinging;
The singing birds with love's delight
    Had hardly time for singing.

Shy summer, looking through the trees
    Where infant leaves were talking,
Smiled softly when she heard the breeze
    Within the wild-wood walking.

Afar the purpled upland stood
    Entranced—a new creation
Still in the spell of solitude
    And silent meditation.

And prayerful as the peace that lies
    About the houms of Yarrow,
I felt the soul that sanctifies
    The touch of every sorrow.

O! You were master of my dream,
    Fond heart, and I obeying
Found voiced in meadow, wood, and stream
    What your leal love was saying.

WILLIAM ALEXANDER.

THE following verses are taken from *The Book of Scottish Song*, edited by Alexander Whitelaw, and published by Blackie & Son, Glasgow, 1875. The editor of the present work regrets that up to the period of its publication he has been unable to obtain any information concerning Alexander. Blackie & Son themselves write that they are quite unable to help him in the matter. Nevertheless, the song has been deemed worthy of a place in this anthology. Alexander is the author of another poem in Blackie's collection—" The Years of Youth."

THE TWEED.

Oh, ha'e ye seen the Tweed while the moon shone bright,
And the stars gemmed the sky wi' their siller light?
  If ye ha'ena seen it, then
  Half its sweets ye canna ken;
  Oh, gae back and look again
   On a shining night!

IN PRAISE OF TWEED.

Oh, ha'e ye seen the Tweed when the cloister and aisle
In the long shadows slept of the mouldering pile?
    Oh, the fondest canna deem
    What that silent scene doth seem
    Till beneath pale Cynthia's beam
        He hath gazed awhile!

Oh, ha'e ye seen the Tweed when the moon's in the cloud—
When the dark waves are rolling both fierce and loud?
    Oh, beware ilk wizard den,
    For, in sooth, ye mayna ken
    What spirit roams the glen
        'Neath their dusky shroud!

Oh, ha'e ye seen the Tweed when the moon's gane down—
When the sun caps ilk hill wi' a gowden crown?
    Oh, ye'd pause in fix'd delight
    As bursts upon the sight,
    'Neath the Eildons, spreading bright,
        The landscape roun'!

But ha'e ye seen the maidens who trip o'er the green
Wi' their tempting lips and their sparkling een?
    Let the Tweed be e'er so fair,
    Still there's something dearer there—
    What were a' the riggs o' Yair
        To my winsome queen?

Oh, ha'e ye seen the Tweed while the moon shone bright,
And the stars gemmed the sky wi' their siller light?
    If ye ha'ena seen it, then
    Half its sweets ye canna ken;
    Oh, gae back and look again
        On a shining night!

From *The Book of Scottish Song.*

W. S. CROCKETT.

Born 1866.

W. S. Crockett, editor of the present work; born at Earlston, June 24, 1866; educated at the parish school; apprenticed to the village chemist, 1881-1885; a student at Edinburgh University, 1885-93; licensed as a probationer of the Church of Scotland, May, 1893; elected minister of Tweedsmuir, June, 1894; editor of *Minstrelsy of the Merse*, 1893; *A Berwickshire Bard*, 1897; *Centenary Edition of Henry Scott Riddell's Poems*, 1898; and author of numerous articles on Border life and literature.

A. G.

AT TWEED'S WELL.

O world that lies outside! O men who dwell
Beyond the confines of these heather hills!
For every charm of rural peace, this Well
Will match its own against a hundred rills;
Yet scarce can one believe that on this mead
We sit beside the source of silver Tweed—
The dear old river of our youth, which fills
The Borderland with beauty and with song
Laden with legend of heroic deed—
Its glens, its holms, and fastnesses among.
Sweet springlet! as your waters course along,
Now here in ocean calm, now there with speed,
Bring to the hearts and homes of Lowland men
Some touch of solace from this upland glen.

THE TWEED.

When Tweed comes gurgling from the hills,
   All heather-crowned and hoary,
From source to surging sea, she fills
   Her winding course with story,
No tract in Scotia's wide domain
Can rival her historic plain.

As on she sweeps, and bends, and bounds
   O'er craggy bed, by shingly shore,
A sweeter song is in her sounds,
   A rarer music in her roar.
A glamour-haunted vale is this
Which the fair river's wavelets kiss.

Each castled steep, each frowning scaur,
   Each lordly hall and hamlet old,
The field that erst hath reeked with war,
   Makes up the tale that now is told,
How hearts heroic battled on
For sake of home and Caledon.

O land of ballads gay and grave,
   Of lover's lilt and tragic scene,
Of warlock's strength to sink or save,
   Of Rhymer and the Fairy Queen,
Gather in one, ye master pens,
The glories of the Lowland glens.

Still let the Mighty Minstrel sing
   His stirring and his deathless lays,
Still let the Shepherd o'er him fling
   His plaid for the old nights and days.
Let them all come—a matchless band,
To view once more their Borderland.

O dear Romance that never dies,
  But lives beyond the Borderland,
Far from the storied soil that lies
  'Tween Berwick bounds and Solway sand,
Still bring to exile in his need
Some touch of home from banks of Tweed.

THE SECRET OF TWEED.

I stood in the uplands to-day,
  How peaceful the pastoral scene,
  Heathered, and gorsy, and green,
Where Tweed first breaks in its silver spray
And bubbling bends to its sea-ward way!

O, rarely sweet, the mystic spell
  That gathered round hill and glen,
  Afar from the haunts of men;
And old-time tales that the legends tell
Were whispered to me by fair Tweed's Well.

Yet all through the stretch of the stream
  To the lap of Berwick Bay
  The light of history lay—
That was the vision; *that* was the dream,
And peerless glory of Border theme.

Sages', wizards', and minstrels' lore
  Passed with the dead centuries—
  Songs, and sufferings, and sighs—
Sweep down with the Tweed's free flood once more,
By castle and crag to sounding shore.

Neidpath, Traquair, holy Melrose,
   Dryburgh's and Kelso's fane,
   Dark Flodden's field of pain
Are quick with the breathing of friends and foes,
Their hopes and struggles, their triumphs and woes.

Not alone, then, beauty of mead,
   Nor charm that Nature imparts,
   Can bind more close to our hearts
The dear stream; but 't is this most indeed—
All the glamour that glows over Tweed.

www.ingramcontent.com/pod-product-compliance
Lightning Source LLC
Chambersburg PA
CBHW020806230426
43666CB00007B/873